Easy
Pruning

THE ROYAL HORTICULTURAL SOCIETY

Easy Pruning

Colin Crosbie

LONDON, NEW YORK, MUNICH, MELBOURNE, DELHI

SENIOR EDITOR Zia Allaway
ACTING SENIOR DESIGNER Rachael Smith
PROJECT EDITOR Emma Callery
PROJECT ART EDITOR Alison Shackleton
MANAGING EDITOR Anna Kruger
MANAGING ART EDITOR Alison Donovan
DTP DESIGNER Louise Waller
PICTURE RESEARCH Lucy Claxton,
Richard Dabb, Mel Watson
PRODUCTION CONTROLLER Rebecca Short

PRODUCED FOR DORLING KINDERSLEY

PHOTOGRAPHY Mark Winwood

First published in Great Britain in 2007 by
Dorling Kindersley Ltd
Penguin Books Ltd
80 Strand
London WC2R 0RL

4 6 8 10 9 7 5 3

A CIP catalogue record for this book is available
from the British Library.

ISBN 9781405316859

Reproduced by Colourscan, Singapore
Printed and bound in Singapore by Star Standard

Discover more at
www.dk.com

Contents

Why and when to prune   6
Achieve beautiful effects by pruning and training
the plants in your garden.

How to prune   22
Learn the basic pruning techniques and choose
the right tools for each job.

Pruning shrubs and trees   44
Discover how to prune woody plants to restrict
their size, and increase fruiting and flowering.

Pruning climbers   76
Find out how to train climbers onto supports,
and prune to encourage more flowers.

Hedges and screens   90
Create beautiful, long-lasting hedges and
screens with careful and timely pruning.

Training and shaping   106
Use the easy steps in this chapter to train roses
on swags and make elegant topiary specimens.

Plant pruning guide   118
Follow the no-nonsense advice on pruning
a wide range of garden plants.

Pruning calendar   146
Check which jobs need to be carried out when
in this easy-to-use seasonal guide.

Index   156
Acknowledgements   160

Why & when to prune

You can achieve many beautiful effects with careful pruning. Some plants are best trimmed lightly to create a naturalistic look, while others can be clipped into elegant formal shapes and topiary. In addition, specific pruning techniques encourage more flowering and fruiting stems to form, increasing the colour and interest in your garden throughout the year. Find inspiration in the gardens featured in this chapter and then follow the advice on how to achieve the ideas that take your fancy.

Informal pruning

Most gardeners love the appearance of a naturalistic, seemingly unpruned garden, brimming with flowers and foliage.

Although the look can be achieved with the minimal amount of work, to create this informal style takes a little practice.

Picture clockwise from left

Wild and free The scene of roses growing in the garden of an old-fashioned country cottage typifies the naturalistic look but, despite appearances, regular pruning has achieved this effect. Long, leggy growths that spoil the shape of the rambler on the wall are cut back into the main body of the plant as soon as they are seen. In autumn or early spring, the plant is given a gentle overall trim to keep its shape. A hard pruning is needed every three to five years.

Beautiful berries Firethorns (*Pyracantha*) make excellent informal, burglar-proof boundary hedges, their thorny stems keeping unwanted visitors at bay. These shrubs come into their own in autumn when covered in berries, and are pruned lightly in spring. Take care not to cut back too much, or you risk losing the berries.

Natural border The success of this scheme is no accident; clever plant selection and a careful pruning regime ensure its natural appeal. If left completely unpruned, one or two plants would become dominant and take over. The silver-leaved *Santolina* and golden sage are lightly trimmed annually, while the *Hypericum* 'Hidcote' is pruned every two or three years to maintain its shape. When in full bloom, the border looks like it has never been pruned.

Colour and texture A good planting combination and the correct plant spacing ensures that this border of *Ceanothus* 'Puget Blue', Mexican orange blossom (*Choisya* 'Aztec Pearl'), and shrubby honeysuckle (*Lonicera nitida* 'Baggesen's Gold') needs only minimal pruning. If vigorous plants had been chosen or this selection had been placed too close together, the border would need much more work. The stems of the *Ceanothus* are shortened annually after flowering (*see p.56*) and the sideshoots of the *Choisya* and shrubby honeysuckle are removed every two or three years to keep them balanced.

Pruning for a formal look

Trees and shrubs can be pruned and trained into many different shapes, and used to great effect in formal designs. Use them as focal points, to create views or backdrops, and to introduce shape and structure into the garden.

Pictures clockwise from top left

Pleached effects Trees such as limes (*Tilia*) or hornbeams (*Carpinus*) can be trained into a structure that resembles a formal hedge on top of a series of straight trunks. This is achieved by training the branches horizontally so that they touch those of the next tree, which is trained in a similar fashion. Each year, the shoots that grow from these branches are pruned hard back to the main branch, resulting in a hedge with a distinctive structure. Use pleached trees to create high hedged effects or as a screen for a formal garden.

Plant patterns A parterre is made from hedges laid out in formal patterns and flowerbeds. The hedges can be of different heights and widths, and the designs intricate or simple. Plants used for a parterre must have a dense growing habit and be tolerant of close clipping, such as box (*Buxus*) or yew (*Taxus*).

Rose cladding Roses have been pruned and trained to cover the wooden supports that frame the view of the formal garden beyond. Mass plantings of hybrid tea and floribunda roses also add to the formal design.

Elegant head This beautiful shrub, *Viburnum rhytidophyllum,* has been pruned to create a stunning focal point. The lowest side stems have been removed, and the top allowed to form a branched head, which appears to float on its elegant "legs". This style of pruning can be practised on many different plants but works best with evergreen shrubs.

Leafy canopy To create this leafy roof structure, several *Sorbus aria* have been trained so that the upper branches arch over to meet in the middle. No branches must be allowed to grow from the trunks, as this would spoil the effect, and those used to form the roof are pruned annually so the structure doesn't lose its shape. This eye-catching canopy takes many years to create.

Pruning to create space

Plants are often pruned to keep them in check, but some delightful effects can be achieved with more imaginative techniques, like clearing lower stems of trees and shrubs to create elegant shapes and extra planting space beneath them.

Pictures from left to right

Training standard bays Lollipop shapes are very useful in a garden's design, as they create interest and structure. Plants that are pruned to create a bare trunk are called "standards". This technique is an excellent way of confining the size of large shrubs, and creating space underneath for a bed of shade-loving plants.

Tiny tree-like wisterias If left unpruned wisterias are large climbers, but it is possible to restrain them with careful pruning. Fruit trees can be trained and pruned in a similar way to fit restricted spaces.

Long-legged birches The most beautiful feature of a silver birch (*Betula*) is its gleaming white stem. To show the trunks off to the best effect, remove the lower branches. This opens up planting spaces beneath, which are perfect for shade-lovers, such as these *Rodgersia*. This pruning technique can be used for any tree or shrub with attractive bark.

Pruning to encourage flowering

Pruning plants correctly can increase the number of flowering shoots produced by the plant, giving you more flowers.

Knowing when and where to prune can make the difference between a poor show and a mass of colour and scent.

Pictures clockwise from left

Purple rain A curtain of scented flowers in late spring, *Wisteria sinensis* needs to be carefully trained and spur pruned each year in late winter to encourage flower bud formation (*see pp.78–9*). *Wisteria* grows very vigorously, so in midsummer shorten the current season's growth by at least half, which also helps encourage the formation of flower buds.

Snowy summer show During early summer *Philadelphus* 'Belle Etoile' is covered with large white scented flowers on arching branches. *Philadelphus* produces flowers on stems that formed the previous summer, so after it has flowered, remove about one-third of the oldest flowering stems, pruning them almost to ground level. Do this annually to help contain the overall size and shape of the plant and encourage plenty of new growth, which will be the flowering stems of the future.

Rose heaven Training a climbing rose, such as this *Rosa* 'Climbing Mrs Sam McGredy', over supports shows off the blooms to their best effect. In late winter or early spring, remove approximately one-third of the oldest stems close to ground level. On the remaining older stems, spur prune all the sideshoots and last year's flowering stems back to two or three healthy buds (*see pp.34–5*) from the main stem. Flowering growths will be produced from all these spurs during the summer. At the same time, tie in strong new growths that formed the previous year, which need this support when they produce flowers.

Less is more *Clematis montana* is a vigorous plant, often grown over buildings and large plant supports. No pruning is required, but it may need trimming after blooming to keep it in check. In fact, some clematis are better left unpruned to encourage maximum flower production. In this instance, pruning reduces the volume of flowers that appear in late spring.

Pruning for colourful stems and bark

Some trees and shrubs produce bold, colourful stems and bark, which can be enhanced by careful pruning to create dazzling effects, especially during the winter when the branches are bare.

Pictures clockwise from top left

Bright highlights Grown for its attractive white peeling bark, the birch *Betula utilis* var. *jacquemontii* is especially effective in the winter when silhouetted against an evergreen backdrop. When the tree is young, use secateurs in early summer to remove the lowest small branches. Then, when the stem has reached the height at which you want the branches to form, allow them to grow but continue to remove the smallest side branches. This will give you a simple yet strong, distinctive branch shape, and a clean white trunk.

Snakeskin decoration Unusual white striations on the green bark of *Acer* 'White Tigress' give rise to the tree's common name – snake-bark maple. To see these markings at their best, create a clear stem of between 1.2 and 1.8m (4 – 6ft) by removing the lowest branches with secateurs annually, until you have the required length of stem.

Show-stopping stems The dogwood *Cornus stolonifera* 'Flaviramea' is grown for its outstanding winter stem interest, with different cultivars ranging from green to orange and dark red. This dogwood is most effective when grown in groups of two or three plants. To achieve the striking winter stem interest, prune the plants annually in early spring using secateurs (*see pp.36–7*).

Burnished bark A member of the cherry family, *Prunus rufa* is grown for its ornamental mahogany coloured bark rather than its flowers, and is ideal for small gardens. The beautiful bark looks best when you can see through the branch structure. To achieve this, remove all the smaller and crossing branches from the main structure.

Beautiful brambles *Rubus cockburnianus* is an ornamental suckering bramble grown for its attractive winter stems, which are white and red in colour. This plant is both a beauty and a beast – the stems are covered in thorns and make an almost impenetrable barrier, so you will need to wear gloves and eye protection when pruning. To attain the attractive winter stem colour, cut the stems to the ground annually in early spring.

Pruning for fruit

Fruit brings welcome colour into the garden as well as edible treats. Fruit bushes and trees require a lot of pruning but the blossom and then colourful and delicious fruit make it all worthwhile.

Pictures clockwise from left

Colourful blueberries The bushes of this popular fruit are great value: they flower in the spring, fruit in the summer, and then provide lovely foliage colour in autumn. Blueberries fruit on branches produced the previous year. Prune the bushes during the winter, removing two or three of the oldest stems each year, as well as any weak, dead, or diseased growths. Also remove any of the lower branches that may lie on the ground when laden with fruit in the summer.

Decorative apples Apple trees are beautiful in blossom and when covered in fruits. When choosing an apple tree for your garden, bear in mind that different varieties grow at different rates, so look for one that suits the size of your garden and the space available. Prune apple trees in the winter to give an open, airy structure (*see pp.72–75*). Do not prune too hard as this stimulates vegetative growth at the expense of flower buds and fruit.

Productive pears Pear trees are suitable for small gardens if trained in a pyramid shape. To keep a tree small reduce the length of the main leader (the tallest stem at the top of the tree) in winter. Also remove any congested growths during the winter when you can clearly see the skeleton of the tree. Then, in late summer reduce the side branches by pruning them back to one leaf bud from the main stem. Pear trees will fruit without any pruning, but they can become too large for a small garden.

Wall-trained espaliers One of the most beautiful and artistic ways to grow an apple tree is to train it as an espalier against a wall, where pairs of branches are trained horizontally from the central stem. Apple espaliers are suitable for small gardens but require great care and maintenance. During the late summer, prune all the sideshoots, taking each one back to the first noticeable leaf above the main horizontal branch. As the plant grows older, the branches that produce fruit will become crowded and will then require thinning in the winter.

What not to prune

All woody plants can be left to develop unpruned, although most will soon become untidy and overgrown. However, there are a few that benefit from no pruning at all, apart from removing dead and diseased stems from time to time.

Pictures clockwise from top left

Rock roses *Cistus* 'Grayswood Pink' is typical of this family of short-lived, summer-flowering shrubs, including x *Halimiocistus*. It pays not to interfere with them, as they do not regenerate easily when cut back. When a shrub dies, dig it up and replace it.

Laburnums All types of laburnum are happiest when left alone. They are naturally small trees that tend not to outgrow their positions, although they will respond to a little pruning in late summer, which is useful when a branch is overhanging a path or driveway. More extensive pruning is likely to ruin a tree's shape and results in a poor flowering display the following spring.

Pieris floribunda This pretty evergreen does not always regenerate if cut back, and because of its neat, round shape covered with dense foliage, pruning is likely to disfigure the plant and leave holes in the canopy. If pruned, a *Pieris* may take many years to regain its shape and flower well.

Rhododendron **'Blue Diamond'** Dense and compact, this rhododendron has small leaves and dazzling flowers in spring. It also grows very slowly, and takes many years to outgrow its position, assuming that it was not planted in an inappropriate, small space. If it does eventually become too big, the best approach is to cut it down and replace it with another one, since it does not respond well to pruning.

Other plants not to prune

- *Callistemon*
- *Clematis montana*
- *Convolvulus cneorum*
- *Daphne x burkwoodii*
- *Daphne cneorum*
- *Edgeworthia*
- *Fothergilla major*
- *Halimiocistus*
- *Prostanthera*
- *Ruscus*
- *Sarcococca*

How to prune

To prune properly you need the right equipment and know-how to make cuts without harming your plants. For example, heavy branches should be cut back in stages to avoid tearing, which can damage the plant and increases the likelihood of infections entering the wound. This chapter lists the essential tools you will need to make clean cuts, and outlines the basic pruning methods, including some more advanced techniques, such as spur pruning, pollarding and coppicing.

Choosing pruning tools

Using the right tool for the right job is one of the most important factors when pruning. Choose your tools carefully and look for good quality products that are safe to use and make sharp, clean cuts that won't damage your plants.

Secateurs There are two types of secateurs: anvil (*above*) and bypass (*right*). The cutting blade of anvil secateurs presses down on to a metal block edge, while the bypass's cutting blade passes the bottom blade in a scissor action. Bypass secateurs give a cleaner cut and are easier to use. Only use secateurs for cutting stems less than 1.5cm (½in) in diameter.

Pruning saw An essential tool, this saw has either a folding or fixed blade which can be replaced when it is worn or damaged. Pruning saws are good for awkward situations.

Long-armed saw Use this saw for cutting small branches above head height. Always wear eye protection and a safety helmet, and save large branches for the professionals.

Bow saw Only use this tool for cutting branches that have already been pruned and removed. The shape makes it unsuitable for use in difficult and awkward situations.

Loppers Often used for pruning branches that are too thick for secateurs – although a pruning saw is the ideal tool – or for reducing the length of branches and stems. When using loppers, don't employ excessive pressure, as you can easily twist and crush the pruned stem.

Long-armed loppers If you need to shorten stems, or remove dead or diseased material that is above head height, this is a useful tool. Never use long-armed loppers to cut stems more than 2.5cm (1in) in diameter as they can be quite difficult to control.

Electric hedge trimmer Useful for cutting most types of hedge. Always work from the bottom to the top, ensure the electric cable is behind you, use an emergency circuit breaker, and never use in damp or wet conditions. Wear ear defenders and always read the instructions before use.

Petrol hedge trimmer Usually much heavier than electric types, petrol trimmers can be tiring to use for long periods. They will saw through most hedges, and are useful for cutting those with thick sideshoots. Always wear ear defenders and read the instructions carefully.

Tool care and safety tips

Using the right pruning tools and correct safety equipment helps to ensure that pruning is safe and enjoyable. You will also protect yourself against accidents if your equipment is well maintained, and extend the life of your tools.

Cleaning secateurs

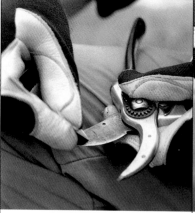

1 When pruning, plant sap dries and sticks to the blades, making them stiff. Scrape off the sap using a piece of metal with a straight edge, such as a metal plant label or penknife.

2 Then rub the blade with steel wool to remove any remaining dried sap and rust or other material. To prevent accidental cuts, wear gloves while cleaning your blades.

3 When the blade is clean, rub on some lubricating oil. This guards against rusting, and keeps the secateurs sharp and clean while they are being stored.

Cleaning pruning saws

1 When you have finished pruning, use a coarse brush to remove any sawdust lodged in the saw's teeth. If this is left it can harden and reduce the saw's cutting ability.

2 Next, use wire wool to rub both sides of the saw blade. This removes dried sap and dirt, which can also make the saw less efficient.

3 Before putting the saw away after cleaning, rub some lubricating oil onto it with a cloth to protect the blade from rusting.

Wear gloves Always wear sturdy gloves when pruning to protect your hands from sharp tools, and from cuts and scratches caused by thorny or sharp-edged plants.

Use protective goggles Protect eyes from dust, sawdust, and plant trimmings, especially when working above head height. Goggles also protect against thorns and shoots.

Keep electric wires behind you When using electric hedge trimmers, ensure that the cable is behind you so you cannot cut through it, and use an emergency circuit breaker.

Pruning your neighbour's plants Before pruning plants that are overhanging your garden, speak to your neighbours. You are more likely to reach an agreement about how much to cut off if you maintain a good relationship. However, branches that overhang your garden are classed by law as trespassing on your air space, and you do have the right to cut them back to your boundary, but no further. The branches that you have cut and any fruit that was on them should then be returned to your neighbour, who is classed as the plant's owner. You are not allowed to enter your neighbour's property, or to lean over it to prune your hedge, without seeking permission first.

Making ladders safe Use a tripod ladder, and ensure it is stable by fully extending the legs. Don't over-stretch or lean out to either side. If possible, ask someone to stand at the bottom.

Using platforms and ladders Before using this equipment, ensure each set of legs is on level ground and adjust if not. Do not over-stretch or lean out too far on either side.

The dangers of chain saws Always call in a qualified tree surgeon to cut down large branches that can be only safely removed with a chain saw. Do not attempt to use one yourself.

Essential pruning jobs

Most pruning tasks are performed annually, but those outlined here need immediate attention and are best tackled as soon as problems are seen.

Crossing and rubbing branches
Branches that have grown too close together and are rubbing against each other is a common problem. If you spot these, remove one of the branches, either the weakest one, or the stem that has suffered the most damage. Branches that rub each other can create open wounds through which disease may enter the plant, causing serious problems.

Removing suckers

A sucker is a vigorous strong growth that emerges from a point low down on a plant, close to the root system. If left, it can choke the plant or reduce its vigour. Such shoots are normally found on plants that have been grafted, such as roses, and usually look quite different to the rest of the plant. If seen early on, remove such a shoot by quickly tugging it away with a gloved hand, or if it has grown too large, remove the shoot using secateurs.

A sucker growing from below the graft (knobbly bulge) on a rose

Cutting out reversed leaves

Reversion is when the leaves of a variegated plant turn pure green. If left to grow, these green shoots, which have greater vigour, can take over and spoil the appearance of the plant. When you see any shoots that are showing signs of reversion, remove them completely using secateurs, and make sure that you prune back to where the shoots are still all variegated. This can be done at any time of the year.

Remove green shoots from variegated plants like *Euonymus* cultivars

Dealing with twin leaders

Twin leaders occur at the top of a tree when two stems of similar vigour are growing close together. Remove the weaker stem using secateurs. If left unpruned, the stems will try to grow away from each other, causing a weakness to develop. One stem may then break away from the tree, causing serious damage. Although this may not happen until the tree is much older, prompt action when the plant is young will prevent future problems.

Limiting frost damage

Buds and young shoots can be damaged when caught by spring frosts. Prune plants back to healthy, unfrosted buds to prevent dieback or diseases from starting at the frosted points. Most plants will then produce new growths lower down the stems. However, on some plants, such as *Hydrangea macrophylla*, frost may damage all the new flower buds produced on the previous season's growth, and you will lose the coming year's blooms (*see p.47*).

| Remove the weaker stem | A single leader has strength |

Hydrangea macrophylla 'Libelle' with frost damage

Cutting out dead and diseased wood

Whenever you see dead or diseased wood on any tree or shrub, remove it immediately. If dead wood is left on a plant, disease can enter more easily and it may move down the stems, attacking healthy growths. Dead wood also looks unsightly. When a tree or shrub has been damaged, its natural defences will eventually form a barrier in the form of a slight swelling between the live and dead wood. In this instance, remove the dead wood above the barrier.

Deadheading to promote flowering

The removal of dead flowerheads can encourage many repeat flowering plants, like roses, to produce more blooms. These dead flowers can be snapped off with the fingers, or removed using secateurs. On some shrubs, like rhododendrons, removing the dead flowers encourages the plant to produce more stems, rather than wasting its energy on making seeds. This enables the plant to produce more flowers the following spring.

| Dead wood on a hornbeam | Coral spot on a branch |

A dying rose bloom can be easily snapped off by hand

Making pruning cuts

Trees, shrubs, and climbers grow in many different ways, and their shoots, buds, and stems may look completely different too. To avoid confusion, before you start pruning, try to identify the position and type of buds and shoots on your plant, and then make your cuts.

Identifying a shoot bud Buds come in many different shapes, sizes, and colours. Some are slight swellings or raised bumps on the stems; others may be a different colour from the rest of the stem, such as rose buds (*see right*). Buds are always produced at the point where leaves are growing, or have previously been attached to the stem. When pruning, you always cut immediately above a bud, which stimulates hormones in the plant to make the bud develop into a new stem.

Pruning to a new shoot A new shoot is normally light green in colour and looks quite obvious, as on the clematis, shown here. New shoots can be quite soft and delicate, and you have to be careful not to damage or break them when pruning back to the new growth.

Pruning to new growth You can recognise the new growth on a plant because it looks much fresher than old wood. When pruning, cut off the old wood just above a new stem, using a sloping cut so that excess moisture runs away from the young growth.

Cutting opposite buds The buds of some plants, such as dogwoods (*Cornus*) and hydrangeas, are opposite each other. Prune immediately above a pair of buds with a flat, straight cut. When the buds grow they will produce two shoots growing in opposite directions from one another.

Cutting alternate buds The buds of plants such as roses and wisteria grow alternately along the stems. Try to prune to a bud that is facing outwards, away from the centre of the plant. Make a sloping cut immediately above the bud, so that excess moisture runs away from the bud.

Using a pruning saw If the stem you intend to prune is thicker than a finger, use a pruning saw to make the cut. Many stems are spoiled by attempting to cut them with incorrect tools. Pruning saws make a much cleaner cut than loppers. Always wear protective gloves.

Shearing When cutting shrubs or hedges with a dense habit, such as yew (*Taxus*) or box (*Buxus*), hand shears are the best tool for the job. Shears are also very useful for trimming lavenders and heathers. Make sure the shears are sharp and clean so you get a good clean cut.

Removing branches

It is very important to remove a branch correctly. Bad or rough cuts can reduce a plant's ability to heal itself, which may then allow disease to enter the wound. Eventually this can cause rotting, reducing the plant's potential lifespan.

Hard to reach branches Branches that are difficult to reach can lead the person who is pruning to take short cuts. Mistakes are more often made when one is attempting to prune from a distance. If the branch that needs to be pruned cannot be reached safely by a ladder, seek the help of a qualified and experienced tree surgeon. If a small branch is not too high, it may be possible to prune it with a long-armed lopper or pruning saw, following the same procedure shown opposite.

Torn branches A heavy branch is likely to tear when being pruned, as its weight will pull down the stem and rip it before you can complete your cut. If you don't have someone to hold the branch while you prune it, shorten it in stages before attempting the final cut. Also make an undercut first (*see Step 1, facing page*), which helps to prevent tearing when you cut through it from above.

Bad cuts Never cut flush to the trunk of the tree as this removes the tree's own healing system. It can look tidy to begin with, but the stem will not heal properly, and the open wound may then allow disease to enter the tree. Cutting branches flush with the trunk is one of the major causes of decay and ultimately death in trees.

How to remove a branch

1 Reduce the weight of a heavy branch by cutting it back in stages to leave a 15cm (6in) stump. Then make the final cut. To prevent tearing, first make an undercut where the branch starts to swell or about 3cm (1¼in) from the trunk.

2 Stop cutting when you are about half way through the branch. Then make another, slightly angled, cut from the top, just behind the crease in the bark where the branch meets the trunk. Ensure the upper cut meets the undercut.

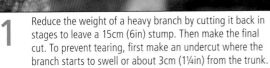

Tip for success

3 This pruning method results in a clean cut, and leaves the plant's healing system intact. The cut surface will soon begin to shrink as the tree produces protective bark, which will eventually cover the exposed area.

When cutting a heavy branch, ask someone to help support the weight when you saw. This helps to prevent tearing. It can also stop the branch swinging or falling, and damaging the plant being pruned or the person who is pruning.

Spur pruning

Spur pruning encourages bud formation on trees, shrubs, and climbers. Where this rose has been spur pruned, it has produced three new stems, each of which will flower.

Spur pruning a rose

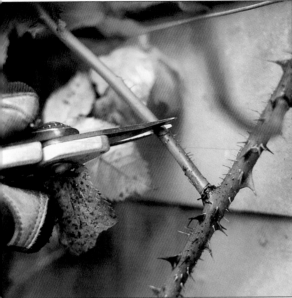

To spur prune a climbing rose, find a healthy side shoot growing from one of the main stems. Count two or three buds from the stem along the shoot. Make an angled cut immediately above this second or third bud, sloping away from it. Repeat further up the main stem.

After pruning, you will be left with short growths, which are described as "spurs". From the buds on these spurs two or three flowering stems will emerge, depending on how many buds were left on the spur.

Spur pruning wisteria

Spur prune wisterias in late winter. Using secateurs, shorten each new shoot that has grown the previous season, so that two or three healthy buds remain. Always make the cut immediately above the outermost bud and sloping away from it.

This picture shows the stems once they have been shortened to two or three buds. The buds on the short spurs will swell to produce flowers or flowering stems in late spring and early summer, producing cascades of sweetly scented purple or white blooms.

Coppicing a dogwood for winter interest

Pruning trees and shrubs down to ground level is known as "coppicing". This technique is used annually for dogwoods (*Cornus*) to encourage masses of colourful winter stems.

1 When pruned annually, dogwoods produce colourful young stems that can be seen clearly when the leaves fall in autumn. To achieve this effect, prune in spring. First, remove all the damaged or diseased stems.

2 Then cut out all weak and thin stems to leave a more open structure. Take breaks from pruning and stand back from the plant. In this way you will be able to identify and remove the spindly stems more easily.

3 Now prune the remaining healthy, strong growths. Take each stem back to the first pair of strong, healthy buds closest to the base, and make a straight cut just above these, as shown.

4 Prune out any crossing and twisting stems. If these are left, the stems arising from them will rub against each other, causing damage. The plant will also become overcrowded and untidy.

5 After pruning, you should be left with a simple, open structure from which a mass of strong, colourful new stems will grow. These will add an excellent decorative feature to the garden the following winter.

Pollarding a willow

Cutting back all the stems of a tree above a clear trunk is called "pollarding", and results in a head of new growth. For winter colour and structure, pollard willows (*Salix*) in spring.

Tip for success

Remove thick stems with a pruning saw rather than loppers, as you are less likely to damage the plant. Do not use secateurs.

1 Start by removing all the weak growths with secateurs. This reduces congestion, and helps to improve access to the pollarded plant, allowing you to prune the strong growths more easily.

2 Spur prune (*see pp.34–35*) the strong growths to one or two buds. Do not be scared to prune out any shoots that are crossing each other or getting in the way.

3 When the pruning is complete, the plant should resemble a lollipop, as shown. This may seem drastic, but willows are very vigorous and will easily put on 1.2–1.4m (4–4½ft) of colourful shoots during the growing season.

Trimming and shaping

The shape of many plants is maintained by trimming. Some plants need to be trimmed just once a year; others, like this cloud-pruned conifer, will need more regular treatment.

Trimming with topiary shears Topiary shears have very sharp blades and work with a scissor action. They are versatile tools, giving a neat cut, and are especially useful for ornate features, producing the fine details required for topiary (*see pp.112–7*). Use these shears when trimming plants that have been trained into intricate and formal shapes. Most of the plants used for topiary have a very dense growth habit, such as yew (*Taxus baccata*), box (*Buxus sempervirens*), or shrubby honeysuckle (*Lonicera nitida*), and do not object to regular clipping.

Using scissors and secateurs Bonsai scissors are used when training bonsai specimens, and slow-growing trees and conifers. Use them to shorten by half the growths of dwarf conifers, such pines (*left*).

Secateurs are suitable for many different pruning and trimming tasks. Use them for snipping off the tips of young trees and shrubs to encourage a bushy growth habit, or to trim and shape small shrubs, such as *Berberis thunbergii*. If you have small groups of *Santolina* or lavender (*Lavandula*), you can use secateurs rather than shears to trim and shape the plants, and to remove their spent flowers.

Sharp shearing Good old garden shears are invaluable for trimming a wide range of plants, from hedges to heathers. Always make sure that your shears are sharp and well maintained. Use them for trimming heathers in early spring, making sure you do not trim back too hard into old brown stems. Also use them for trimming lavender (*Lavandula*) hedges in spring (*see pp.64–5*), and for removing the dead flowers in the summer. If you have small evergreen or deciduous hedges, shears are the ideal tool for trimming them too (*see pp.98–9*).

Minimal pruning

Many young plants and shrubs, such as this *Daphne bholua* 'Jacqueline Postill', produce long, leggy growths in the spring. Trim them and the resulting bushier plant will produce more flowers.

1 In early summer, *Daphne* starts to produce many long growths at the ends of its main stems. These can give the plant an untidy and leggy appearance.

2 Using secateurs, shorten the leggy growths by 15–20cm (6–8in). Always prune immediately above a leaf bud with an angled, slanting cut, as shown.

Pruning young plants

3 Continue to work around the plant. Trimming the stems like this encourages bushier growth, and all the new stems will produce flowers in the winter. It also helps to keep the plant smaller and more compact.

Where the growths are softer on young plants, you can pinch out the tips with your thumb and forefinger. It is good practice to do this with many young shrubs because it helps to produce a compact, well-branched structure.

Pruning shrubs and trees

Many woody plants need regular pruning to keep them in shape and to encourage greater numbers of flowers and fruit to form. In this chapter, step-by-step sequences show you how to prune a range of trees and shrubs, techniques that you can apply to similar plants in your garden. The main rule of thumb, which applies to most shrubs, is to cut back those that flower early in the year immediately after they have finished blooming, and to prune shrubs that flower from midsummer onwards in late winter or early spring. Rose pruning is also described in detail here, and there are simple steps showing how to prune an apple tree.

Pruning hydrangeas

Hydrangea paniculata flowers in late summer on stems it has made that same year. To keep the plants compact prune in early spring to promote new flowering wood. This also encourages larger flower panicles in the summer.

Hydrangea paniculata is an elegant plant with wonderful large cone-like flowerheads. Most have white flowers but there are also cultivars that are tinged with pink. They make excellent shrubs for the late summer garden.

1 In late winter or early spring, prune last season's stems to one or two buds from their base. Also take out any dead, diseased, crossing and weak branches.

2 Any large, unhealthy branches should be cut back into healthy wood or to the base using a pruning saw. This prevents disease from spreading to the rest of the plant and promotes the growth of new vigorous stems.

3 After pruning, you will be left with an open framework of branches. These will produce a mass of growth during the summer and an abundance of beautiful white flowers.

Hydrangea macrophylla, or mophead hydrangea, flowers in summer from buds that have already been set the previous summer. These buds are prone to frost damage in the spring months, and plants need careful pruning.

Hydrangea macrophylla produces sumptuous large flowerheads in blue, pink or white during the summer months, before *H. paniculata*. To ensure a good display, the developing flower buds need some frost protection throughout winter.

1 The hydrangea's old flowerheads help to protect the delicate new flower buds from frosts, so leave them on the plant during the winter months. The dried flowers also add structure and interest to the winter garden.

2 When the danger of hard frost has passed in late spring, remove the flowerheads by pruning the stems back to a pair of healthy buds, as shown.

3 Do not be tempted to prune too hard as this will remove many of the flower buds, which will have already formed on the stems that grew the previous year. New stems that grow in the coming year will bloom the following summer.

How to prune a smoke bush

Grown for their outstanding summer and autumn foliage, and tiny, cloud-like flowers, smoke bushes (*Cotinus*) are best pruned annually in the spring.

Other plants to prune this way

- *Catalpa bignonioides*
- *Cotinus coggygria*
- *Rhus chinensis*
- *Rhus typhina*
- *Sambucus nigra*
- *Weigela* 'Praecox Variegata'
- *Weigela* Wine and Roses

Foliage effects

Pruning hard encourages the plant to produce larger, more decorative leaves, although you may lose the smoke-like blooms.

1 Mature smoke bushes can outgrow their allotted location and suffer from dieback. Both problems are easily remedied by cutting plants back hard in the spring before the leaves appear.

2 First, remove any dead growth using a pruning saw. Also cut out diseased stems, taking them back to healthy growth. When removing large branches, cut them back in stages to ensure they do not tear (*see pp.32–33*).

3 To keep a cotinus small and compact, cut back all of the taller branches to about 60cm (2ft). Prune to healthy wood, which you can identify by checking that it is green in colour beneath the bark, and make sloping cuts.

4 Continue around the plant until you are left with a core structure of stems, each no higher than 60cm (2ft). New growth will soon start to sprout, resulting in plenty of fresh foliage that will provide exciting autumn colour.

Pruning witch hazel

With their fragrant, spidery flowers, witch hazels (*Hamamelis*) are wonderful shrubs in winter, but if left unpruned, they can become too large for a small garden.

Tip for success

Prune witch hazels just as the flowers are fading but before the leaves unfurl. Cut just above a healthy young sideshoot.

1 To reduce the size of this plant, in early spring prune back the taller branches by 30–50cm (12–20in). Try to keep in mind the overall shape you are aiming to achieve.

2 While pruning, step back occasionally to look at what you have cut out, and what still needs to be done. Always prune out old stems, leaving healthy young growth.

Tip for success

3 Occasionally you may find some crossing branches in the centre of the bush that are difficult to reach. If a branch is awkwardly positioned, it may be easier to cut upwards from below the branch.

If you are not sure how much to remove, reduce the length of the stems a little at a time. Stand back, and then prune more if needed, until you have created an attractive overall shape.

How to prune shrubby honeysuckle

Prune winter-flowering shrubs, such as *Lonicera x purpusii* 'Winter Beauty', in early summer. Remove the oldest flowering stems to encourage new, strong shoots to grow from the base.

Tip for success

It is much easier to use a pruning saw to cut through branches that are too thick for either loppers or secateurs.

1 First, reduce one-third of the oldest stems on the plant. Use loppers to cut back their length by about half, thereby decreasing the weight of the stem and preventing tearing, before you make the final cut closer to the ground.

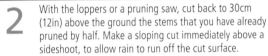

2 With the loppers or a pruning saw, cut back to 30cm (12in) above the ground the stems that you have already pruned by half. Make a sloping cut immediately above a sideshoot, to allow rain to run off the cut surface.

3 Using secateurs, shorten the tallest of the new stems, which may be over 1.8m (6ft) high, by several centimetres (inches). This encourages buds further down the plant to shoot, creating a bushier plant with more flowers.

4 When you have finished pruning, you should still have some older stems that will produce flower buds the following winter. The strong young growths coming from the base will now have more room to develop.

Hard pruning a camellia

Evergreen shrubs, such as camellias, that have outgrown their position can be hard pruned in late spring or summer, just after they have finished flowering.

Other plants to prune this way

- *Aucuba japonica*
- *Elaeagnus pungens*
- *Erica arborea*
- *Escallonia*

- *Fatsia japonica*
- *Prunus laurocerasus*
- *Prunus lusitanica*
- *Viburnum tinus*

New growth

A year after pruning the plant will have produced a mass of young stems but may not flower for a further two or three years.

1 This plant has outgrown its location and now needs to be cut back hard. Camellias respond very well to severe pruning, a task best performed immediately after they have finished flowering in late spring or early summer.

2 Use a pruning saw to reduce the height of the plant. To prevent tearing, cut back large, heavy branches in stages, rather than cutting off long sections. (*see pp.32–3*).

3 Loppers are ideal tools for pruning back awkwardly placed side stems, allowing you to reach them more easily. But the final cut close to the main branch must be made using a pruning saw, as it gives a cleaner cut.

4 Aim to reduce the plant height to about 60cm (24in). By the time you have finished, the camellia will resemble a small wooden stump, but it will not take long for new shoots to start growing (*see opposite page*).

Cutting back California lilacs and philadelphus

Most California lilacs (*Ceanothus*) have vivid blue flowers in early summer. If left unpruned, they can become large and untidy, but if cut back too severely, the plant will not regenerate. Prune immediately after flowering is finished.

1 Here you can see an evergreen *Ceanothus* in full bloom in early summer. To maintain its compact shape, it will need to be lightly pruned later in the summer, after it has finished flowering .

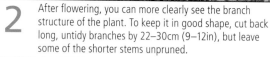

2 After flowering, you can more clearly see the branch structure of the plant. To keep it in good shape, cut back long, untidy branches by 22–30cm (9–12in), but leave some of the shorter stems unpruned.

3 Use secateurs to prune the branches, and make each cut immediately above a leaf bud. This will encourage the plant to produce growths from below the cut, resulting in a compact branching structure.

4 After pruning, the overall size of the plant is reduced, but it has not been cut back too severly, which would weaken it. If pruned like this annually, the *Ceanothus* will remain neat and bushy, suitable for a small garden.

Philadelphus has white scented flowers in early summer. Prune the plant after flowering to encourage the formation of new growths, which will bear flowers in the future. An annual prune also helps to contain the size of the plant.

1 In early summer, mock orange (*Philadelphus*) is a mass of white scented flowers. As soon as flowering has finished, cut back about a quarter of the oldest flowering stems to 15cm (6in) above the ground .

2 Cutting back hard some of the oldest stems promotes the formation of new shoots below the pruning cut, but do not be tempted to remove all the old stems, as this will reduce the volume of flowers the following summer.

3 Check the remaining old stems for young growths. These are best shortened rather than being hard pruned. Take off the top third of these young stems, and prune them back to new wood (*see p.30*).

4 Finally, trim the tips of any strong young stems that are already present in the plant – some may be as tall as 2.5m (8ft). This encourages them to branch lower down, which results in more flowers.

How to prune a patio rose

Patio roses are small, repeat-flowering plants that can be grown in borders or containers. Prune them in early spring to encourage a mass of new shoots that will flower in the summer.

Tip for success

As well as pruning your rose every year, encourage it to keep flowering for longer by removing the blooms as they fade.

1 The aim of pruning is to reduce the plant's height by one-quarter to a half and to create an open shape. Cut back the outer stems, and then remove dead, diseased, and damaged growths, plus any weak and crossing stems.

2 Always prune above a strong outward-facing bud if possible. Ensure that the cuts are sloping so that rainfall runs away from the bud, reducing the chance of it rotting.

3 This strong stem is being cut back by one-half, which will encourage many strong flowering shoots to grow from it in the forthcoming summer.

4 As well as producing more flowering stems, the resulting simple framework allows air movement, which reduces the incidence of fungal diseases. Feed and mulch roses after pruning to further encourage healthy growth.

How to prune a shrub rose

Most modern shrub roses are repeat flowering and do not need to be pruned as hard as some roses, since they flower on older stems. Prune your shrub roses in early spring.

1 The aim of pruning a shrub rose is to create a strong structure and to remove congested stems that were produced the previous year. This improves air flow through the plant, which helps to prevent fungal diseases.

2 Cut off any dead, damaged, or diseased branches. Then remove any weak shoots not strong enough to support new flower growths. Also prune a few of the oldest stems down to the ground.

3 Reduce healthy main stems by a quarter, and prune some of the sideshoots by just a few centimetres (inches). Always cut above a healthy bud that faces outwards, away from the centre of the plant, if possible.

4 The pruned plant should be reduced in height by about a quarter, and have a strong, open, structure that appears uncluttered in the centre. By midsummer the plant should be covered in beautiful blooms.

Pruning other types of roses

Different types of roses have different pruning needs. Identify your roses and then follow these guidelines to ensure yours produce their best show.

Hybrid tea roses

This group of roses normally flowers more than once during the summer months. They respond well to hard pruning in early spring. First remove all dead, damaged, diseased, weak, and crossing stems, and then prune out the oldest stems, taking them back to the ground. Leave between three and five young, strong stems, which should be pruned to a height of 15cm (6in) above the soil. As a guide, stand your secateurs on the ground, and as these are normally about 15cm (6in) long, they will show you how far to prune back the stems. Always make a sloping cut above an outward-facing bud, if possible. In late autumn or early winter, reduce the height of the stems by one-third to reduce the risk of wind rocking the plant and damaging the roots.

Old garden roses

These roses normally have one flush of flowers each year. Prune in early spring, first removing any dead, damaged, diseased, weak, and crossing branches. They do not need severe pruning: aim to reduce the size of the plant by one-third. Always make a sloping cut above an outward-facing bud. In the autumn, cut back the stems by one-third to reduce the risk of wind rocking the plant and damaging the roots.

Examples of old garden roses

- *Rosa* 'Blanche Double de Coubert'
- *Rosa* 'Boule de Neige'
- *Rosa* 'Charles de Mills'
- *Rosa* 'De Rescht'
- *Rosa* 'Fantin-Latour'
- *Rosa* 'Frau Dagmar Hartopp'
- *Rosa* 'Louise Odier'
- *Rosa* 'Madame Isaac Pereire'
- *Rosa* 'Madame Pierre Oger'
- *Rosa* 'Maiden's Blush'
- *Rosa mundi*
- *Rosa rugosa*
- *Rosa rugosa* 'Alba'
- *Rosa* 'Souvenir de la Malmasion'
- *Rosa* 'William Lobb'

Examples of hybrid tea roses

- *Rosa* Alexander
- *Rosa* 'Blessings'
- *Rosa* Dawn Chorus
- *Rosa* 'Deep Secret'
- *Rosa* Elina
- *Rosa* Freedom
- *Rosa* Ingrid Bergman
- *Rosa* 'Just Joey'
- *Rosa* Lovely Lady
- *Rosa* Paul Shirville
- *Rosa* Peace
- *Rosa* Remember Me
- *Rosa* Savoy Hotel
- *Rosa* 'Silver Jubilee'
- *Rosa* Tequila Sunrise
- *Rosa* Troika
- *Rosa* Warm Wishes

Floribunda roses

Floribundas are repeat-flowering roses that produce clusters of blooms during the summer months. Pruning is very similar to hybrid tea roses, but not quite as hard. First, remove all dead, damaged, diseased, weak, and crossing stems. Your aim is to leave a framework of between six and eight of the strongest, youngest stems. Prune them to a height of between 20–30cm (8–12in), always make a sloping cut just above an outward-facing bud, if possible. In the autumn or early winter, reduce the height of the stems by one-third to reduce the risk of damage when wind rocks the plant and disturbs its root system.

Examples of floribunda roses

- *Rosa* 'Arthur Bell'
- *Rosa* 'English Miss'
- *Rosa* Fascination
- *Rosa* Fellowship
- *Rosa* 'Fragrant Delight'
- *Rosa* Iceberg
- *Rosa* Memento
- *Rosa* Pretty Lady
- *Rosa* 'Princess of Wales'
- *Rosa* Queen Elizabeth
- *Rosa* Remembrance
- *Rosa* Sexy Rexy
- *Rosa* Sunset Boulevard
- *Rosa* Tall Story
- *Rosa* The Times Rose
- *Rosa* Trumpeter

Extending flowering

Deadhead repeat-flowering roses throughout the summer to encourage them to bloom for a longer period. By removing the flowers, you prevent the plant from using its energy to form seed and stimulate it to produce more flowers instead. The easiest way to do this, and the way now practised in many large gardens, is to bend the stem just below the old flower, as shown, until it snaps off. The plant will soon start forming new flower buds. Alternatively, use secateurs to remove the flower and about 15cm (6in) of growth. The plant will then form more flowers buds, but it normally takes longer than the "snapping off" method.

Shearing lavender

Lavender (*Lavandula*) is a beautiful, aromatic shrub that can be grown on its own or as a low growing, colourful hedge. To maintain a good shape, it is best sheared twice a year.

Tip for success

After flowering, remove all the old flowerheads with secateurs. This stops the plant from putting all its energy into making seed.

1 To keep your lavender plants young, bushy, and healthy, cut them back in late winter or early spring using clean, sharp hedge shears.

2 Shear the lavender as close as possible without cutting into the old wood. This is very important as the old wood does not regenerate, which means that if you cut into it no new shoots will grow from the stems.

3 Here, you can see how the lavender has been cut just above where the new green shoots meet the old, brown wood. Shear to this point, and work systematically along and around the hedge, keeping it as level as possible.

4 This form of pruning encourages the lavender to become very bushy, and to produce a greater volume of flowers. The hedge then needs to be pruned again as the flowers fade in summer (see Tip for success opposite).

How to prune wall shrubs

Euonymus fortunei cultivars are vigorous plants that will grow even in poor soil. They often form rounded shrubs, but will also grow vertically, the variegated forms creating bright cladding for walls and fences. Prune plants in late spring.

1 As with all variegated plants, it is important to remove any growths that are showing signs of reversion (*see p.28*), where stems of all-green leaves appear. Cut these back to variegated foliage using secateurs as soon as possible.

2 Using secateurs, cut back to a suitable length any very long growths that are hanging away from the wall and causing the plant to loose its neat shape.

3 To keep it neat and bushy, trim over the whole plant with hedging shears. Keep one eye on the overall shape to ensure you trim it as evenly as possible.

4 Remove any growths that are growing towards or into gutters or over doors and windows. When you have finished, the plant should resemble a closely clipped hedge growing against its supporting wall or fence.

Garrya elliptica is a useful evergreen shrub that produces long, pendulous catkins in the winter. It prefers to grow against the shelter of a wall for support and protection, and is best pruned in the spring, as the catkins are fading.

1 Any plant occasionally needs a prune to prevent it from growing too tall or wide. For a shrub trained against a wall, it also prevents it from becoming too heavy and pulling or falling away from its support.

2 Start by pruning the longest horizontal branches to reduce the width of the plant. Always make the cuts above a leaf bud or stem shoot to encourage new, fuller growth during the coming year.

3 Once you have trimmed the horizontal branches, start pruning the tall, vertical stems. Cut them back to a height that is appropriate for the position of the plant.

4 If the plant is pruned carefully, it should still retain its natural shape afterwards. The new growths that appear as a result of pruning will produce a good show of catkins the following winter.

How to prune a mahonia

When evergreens such as this mahonia have outgrown their allotted space they can be pruned back severely from midwinter to early spring, after flowering has finished.

Tip for success

To keep plants short and bushy and to encourage greater flower production, remove flowerheads immediately after flowering.

1 Prune back tall stems, removing a little at a time, rather than cutting back the whole growth in one go (*see pp.32–33*). At this stage cut the stems to about 60cm (2ft) high, keeping in mind the plant's balanced shape as you prune.

2 Once you have cut back the tall growths, look to see where you can make your final pruning cuts. At the same time, remove any damaged, diseased, or crossing stems, and cut out any old growths to leave 5 or 6 strong stems.

3 Cut back the remaining young healthy stems so that they are 30–40cm (12–16in) above the ground. If possible, ensure that all the cuts you make are slightly sloping to encourage the rain to run off.

4 Later in the year a mass of young shoots will grow from these shortened stems. The plant may not flower until two years after a severe pruning like this. Thereafter, to keep it bushy, follow the Tip for success (*see facing page*).

Pruning a holly bush

A well-shaped holly (*Ilex*) can provide a wonderful structural focal point in the garden all year round. To maintain their shape, it is best to prune holly bushes in early spring.

Holly hedge

Holly has thick, chunky growth so holly hedges are best trimmed in late summer using a petrol or electric hedge cutter.

1 To ensure that this young holly remains an attractive feature in the garden, it needs to be pruned annually, first to form a conical shape, and then to retain it.

2 Remove some of the lower branches to create space under the bush and a short, clear stem. This is known as "lifting the skirt" and produces a bolder appearance.

3 If two branches are growing closely together at the top of the plant and causing it to lose its conical shape, cut the weaker one – or the stem that is least vertical – above a shoot that is growing in line with the conical outline.

4 Work all around the bush, trimming back any branches that are too long, until you have a conical shape that is symmetrical and pleasing to the eye.

How to prune an apple tree

When carefully managed, an apple tree is highly ornamental, providing decorative blossom in the spring and a wealth of colourful fruit in the autumn. Prune in summer or winter.

1 Start by removing any branches that are crowding the centre of the tree. This will allow air to circulate, which reduces the risk of fungal infections during the summer. Also remove any dead, diseased, or damaged branches.

2 Cut the branches back to the collar (*see pp.32–33*). Make clean cuts with a sharp saw to reduce the risk of infection entering the wounds. Don't prune too hard, as it stimulates leafy growth at the expense of flowers and fruit.

3 Only reduce the height of the tree yourself if you can reach the top easily. Cut back any long branches by a half to one-third, or to a suitable side branch that, if possible, faces outwards to prevent any crossing branches.

4 When pruning back to a side branch, make an undercut first, and saw half way through the stem. Then make the final cut from above, sloping away from the side branch, to meet the undercut. This prevents the branch from tearing.

How to prune an apple tree *continued*

5 The sloping cut you make after removing a branch (*above*) allows moisture and rainfall to drain off the cut surface, reducing the risk of rotting. The remaining side branch should also point outwards.

6 Shorten any long, thin, whippy growths by cutting them back to short branches or spurs with a pair of secateurs. This encourages flower bud formation from these branches (*see pp.34–35*).

7 Where pruning cuts have been made in previous years, remove any short, weak, or crowded stems growing around the wound. These are of no use to the tree and divert energy from the main branches and flower stems.

8 Remove all branches that are crossing or are starting to grow from the outside of the tree into the centre. This helps to prevent branches from rubbing against each other in future, thereby reducing the risk of disease.

9 Continue to work around the tree, removing unwanted branches and taking care to make clean cuts. Step back from the tree to ensure you have created a balanced, simple framework, with an uncongested centre.

Pruning climbers

Climbing plants have special pruning requirements, although the timing is usually the same as for trees and shrubs. The most widely grown climbers are clematis and roses, and both will reward you with many months of colourful flowers if pruned correctly. Clematis fall into three pruning groups, and are categorized according to when they flower – look at the plant labels to discover which groups yours fall into. Each group has its own pruning method, and all three are clearly explained here. Detailed advice on pruning climbing and rambling roses is also presented as simple step-by-steps to help you to get the most from your plants.

How to prune wisteria

Wisterias are beautiful plants for training up house walls and other structures. Prune these large, vigorous climbers twice a year, once in summer to keep the plant in check, and again in winter to help stimulate flowering.

Summer pruning

1 Wisterias are vigorous plants and during the summer after they have flowered, the plants produce very long tendril-like shoots that can block house windows or paths, or swamp their supporting structures.

2 To keep your wisteria tidy, reduce these shoots by two-thirds after the flowers have faded. This process may have to be repeated several times during the summer months as the plant continues to grow.

Winter pruning

1 In late winter, when the leaves have dropped, you will be able to see the effects of your summer pruning. The pruned stems will have developed new growth, which will look lighter in colour than older wood.

2 Spur prune (*see pp.34-35*) all the stems that you pruned in the summer back to two or three healthy buds. These buds will then swell to become flower buds in spring.

3 Also remove any stems that are growing into the eaves of the house, under roofing tiles, or around drainpipes. If left, they could cause damage to the house structure.

4 Ensure all stems are tied to sturdy wires on the house or plant supports, as wisteria is not self-clinging. The plant will look quite naked, but the buds will develop into a wall of scented flowers in late spring or early summer.

Cutting back clematis

Admired for their beautiful flowers, you can use clematis for an almost year-round show. They are divided into three groups, each with different pruning needs, so work out which one yours belongs to and follow these guidelines.

Group 1

Group 1 clematis are vigorous plants, and include *C. montana*, *C. alpina* and *C. armandii*. Flowering in late spring on the previous year's growth, they require very little pruning. Prune lightly immediately after they have flowered to contain their size, and remove dead, diseased, or damaged growth (*see p.81 for more details*).

Group 2

This group of early summer-flowering clematis have large flowers that are produced from the previous year's growth. Many will also produce a second flush of flowers in late summer. Group 2 clematis require a light prune in early spring. Prune back the stems to a pair of healthy buds (*see p.81 for more details*).

Group 3

Group 3 clematis include the small-flowered viticella and texensis types, *C. tangutica* and its cultivars, and some large-flowered hybrids. They bloom from midsummer to autumn on new season's growth and require hard pruning in early spring (*see p.82*), or you can prune them more lightly (*see p.83*).

Clematis montana (Group 1)

Clematis 'Nelly Moser' (Group 2)

Clematis 'Etoile Violette' (Group 3)

Clematis 'Frances Rivis' (Group 1)

Clematis 'H.E.Young' (Group 2)

Clematis tangutica (Group 3)

Pruning after planting

Help all groups of clematis to get established by pruning them after planting in spring, or in their first year immediately after flowering. Reduce the plant's height by one half, ensuring that you prune above a pair of healthy buds. This encourages the plant to produce growths from all the buds on the stem below the pruning cut, which will ultimately give you a much stronger plant. It also encourages root production, helping to develop strong, healthy growth. Take care when handling any clematis as the shoots can be very brittle.

Pruning Group 1

Immediately after flowering, give Group 1 clematis a light trim to help contain the size of the plant and to keep it looking tidy. Prune strong, leggy new season's growths, cutting above a pair of healthy buds. This will also help to show off the plant's attractive fluffy seedheads, but don't prune too hard or you will remove them. If a plant becomes too large, occasionally prune all stems back to 15cm (6in) from the ground in early spring. Montanas may not recover from this treatment, so only carry out drastic pruning if you have no choice.

Pruning Group 2

Prune Group 2 clematis in early spring when the buds are already in growth and new stems are visible. Work from the top of the plant, pruning each stem back to the first pair of healthy buds or growths. Remove any dead, diseased, or damaged wood. New growths will appear along the pruned stems, and these produce the flowers in early summer. If the plant has outgrown its site, hard prune all stems to 15cm (6in) from the ground in early spring. It may then not flower during the forthcoming summer, or it may bloom later in the season.

Prune above a pair of healthy buds

Cut away excess growth in spring

Prune lightly back to new growth

New growth soon emerges

Pruning helps to show off seedheads

Buds open below the pruning cuts

How to prune a Group 3 clematis

The late-flowering *Clematis* x *jouiniana* is extremely vigorous, and is suitable for clothing large supports or growing through substantial shrubs or small trees. As it belongs to pruning Group 3, it requires hard pruning in early spring.

1 This clematis has been grown over a large pyramid support made from birch twigs. Start pruning by removing all the loose growths that are covering the support.

2 Once all the stems have been removed from the support, you will have better access to the base of the plant. Prune back all long growths to give a manageable clump of short stems before making your final cuts.

3 Prune the growths hard back to one or two buds from the ground, as shown. Always make straight cuts just above a pair of healthy buds to reduce the risk of dieback.

4 You will be left with a mound of growths about 15cm (6in) high. To encourage healthy growth, add a little fertilizer and mulch. The plant will then grow 2–3m (6–10ft) and will be covered in flowers during late summer.

Lightly pruning late-flowering Group 3 clematis, such as this *Clematis tangutica*, encourages the plant to flower earlier.

Follow these simple steps to create a cascade of beautiful yellow nodding flowers throughout the summer.

1 In early spring and starting at the top of the plant, lightly prune back the main stems to fit the shape of the support. As with any pruning, also remove dead, damaged, or diseased stems as you work.

2 Then lightly prune the side stems back to the plant support. This will maintain the shape of the plant and encourage strong new growths that will flower in the summer. Make sure all cuts are made above two buds.

3 If there are strong young growths coming from the base of the plant, tie them in to the rest of the clematis so that they will not wave about in the wind and get damaged – clematis stems are brittle and easily broken.

4 When you have finished, the clematis should look as if it has had a light haircut, since you have just trimmed it back to the shape of the supporting structure.

Cutting back honeysuckle and ivy

Climbing honeysuckles (*Lonicera*) are grown for their beautifully scented flowers. Allow them to scramble over shrubs and trees in the garden, or encourage them to climb up supports, such as fences or trellises.

Climbing honeysuckles are easy to grow, and produce masses of sweetly scented blooms in summer. As they age, plants can become woody at the base, and look untidy and overgrown. Keep them in check and flowering prolifically by pruning regularly.

1 In spring, contain the size of a honeysuckle by removing long straggly growths and reducing the overall height of the plant by 30–50cm (12–20in).

2 Remove old, dead, damaged, or diseased stems. If your plant is very overgrown, cut all the stems back to about 15cm (6in) from the ground. New shoots will soon appear from the base, but you may lose the flowers that year.

3 Unless you gave the plant a hard prune, by late summer it will produce an even covering of flowers. If the plant has put on a lot of growth and is looking untidy, trim it again immediately after flowering has finished.

Ivies are versatile evergreen climbers that will grow in sun or shade, and adhere to almost any support or surface. In late spring or early summer, prune these vigorous plants to contain their spread, and to prevent stems clogging gutters.

1 The aim of pruning here is to reduce the plant's spread over the fence and to remove it from the tree trunk in front. Ivy can collect a lot of dust and dirt, so wear a dust mask when pruning if this affects you.

2 Working from the top of the fence panel, pull away long lengths of ivy. When you are happy with the amount removed, cut off the stems with secateurs. Also cut and pull away any ivy growing on tree trunks or other plants.

3 Remove ivy growing up walls and into house guttering. When removing ivy from walls you will reveal marks left by the roots, which help the ivy to cling to the surface. Use a stiff brush to remove the root residue.

4 The ivy has been cut back from the top of the fence by about 45cm (18in) to allow room for regrowth. It has also been removed from the tree trunk, resulting in a less cluttered and lighter part of the garden.

How to prune a rose on a tripod

Climbing roses, such as this *R.* 'White Cockade', can be trained over a wooden tripod to create a lovely focal point in a small space. Prune the rose in autumn or early spring.

Before pruning

The plant is a mass of stems, some of which are old and must be removed, while the younger stems need to be tied in.

1 Start by removing the rose stems from the tripod support. Cut all the ties that are holding the rose to the support, and then carefully unwind the stems, working down from the top of the plant.

2 Cut out any dead, damaged, or diseased wood. Then remove about one in three of the oldest stems by pruning them close to the base of the plant. Leave enough stems unpruned to cover the tripod.

3 With the unpruned older stems that you left to cover the tripod, spur prune the previous season's flowering stems (*see pp.34–35*), and tie them in. These spurs will produce flowering stems in the forthcoming summer.

4 Tie back the remaining young flexible stems using garden twine. To give the best coverage over the tripod, tie some in a clockwise and others in an anticlockwise direction.

Pruning rambling and climbing roses

Ensure a mass of flowers each year by pruning rambling and climbing roses during the autumn while their stems are still quite flexible. If you don't have time in autumn, these roses can also be pruned in late winter or early spring.

1 Remove one in three of the oldest flowering stems. These growths will be quite thick and should be cut back to almost ground level using a pruning saw or loppers.

2 Use sharp secateurs to spur prune the previous summer's flowering stems back to two or three healthy buds (*see pp.34–35*). These will then produce flowering stems during the forthcoming summer months.

Summer maintenance

3 Use garden twine or special rose ties to tie in all the stems. Bending flexible stems over and tying them onto horizontal supports or wires encourages the production of more flowering growths.

Do not attempt to prune a rambling rose in summer. Just tie in and support the long, strong new growths that have been produced, so that they are not damaged or broken. These are the stems that you will be cutting back when pruning and training in autumn.

This climbing rose has been carefully pruned and trained along horizontal wires that have been attached to the wall with vine eyes. Use galvanised wire and fix it at about 30cm (12in) intervals up the wall before planting your rose.

1 Cut all the ties that are holding the rose to the wires and pull the stems away from the wall. Remove one in three of the oldest flowering stems. Do not remove any of the strong new growths produced from the base of the plant.

2 Spur prune last season's flowering stems back to two or three healthy buds (*see pp.34–35*) to encourage them to produce more flowering stems in the months ahead.

3 Tie all the remaining growths back onto the wires, and try to cover as much of the wall as possible. You may find some of the stems cross over one another but this won't be a problem as long as they don't rub.

4 Step back from time to time to ensure that you have tied the stems in a fan shape over the wall. By the time summer arrives, the plant will have produce more stems covered in leaves and flowers and the wall will be hidden.

Hedges and screens

Much admired for their natural good looks and value to wildlife, hedges are back in vogue. Another reason for their increasing popularity is that many hedging plants require very little maintenance. Beautiful beech and hornbeam hedges, for example, require just one cut each year, and a smooth, sheer yew screen can be achieved with a trim or two in the summer. However, there are other fast-growing types, most notably Leyland cypresses, that make great hedges if cut at least twice a year, but are best avoided if you're looking for an easy life. This chapter helps you to select a hedge that's right for you and your garden, and explains how and when to prune it.

Hedge pruning requirements

All hedges need pruning and trimming to keep them in good shape, but while some require just one clip per year, others demand more frequent cuts, so choose your hedging carefully by checking different plants' needs.

Fast-growing Leyland cypress This vigorous evergreen will soon reach a great height if left unpruned. It makes an excellent dense hedge, providing shelter and privacy, but must be trimmed regularly to keep it within bounds.

Decorative hornbeam Although hornbeam (*Carpinus*) is deciduous, many of the copper coloured dead leaves stay on the hedge in winter, if trimmed in late summer. Prune in the same way as beech (*see pp.100–101*).

Flowering rose hedge *Rosa rugosa* is a popular hedge, grown for its scented early summer flowers and large red hips in autumn. Its thorny stems also provide security. Prune rose hedges in late winter or early spring.

Tough berberis Bearing a profusion of pretty flowers and berries, but armed with ferocious spines, a *Berberis darwinii* hedge makes a secure boundary. Prune hard back into shape during the summer; it recovers well.

Formal and elegant For a neat, tidy hedge, choose a plant that tolerates frequent clipping to maintain its shape. Evergreen conifers, box (*Buxus*), and some deciduous species like hornbeams make perfect formal hedges.

PLANTS IDEAL FOR HEDGING

PLANT	TYPE	FEATURE	USE	WHEN TO CLIP
Berberis darwinii	informal evergreen	flowers, berries	boundary	midsummer
Buxus sempervirens (box)	formal evergreen	foliage	edging	early or midsummer
Carpinus (hornbeam) and *Fagus* (beech)	formal/informal evergreen	foliage	boundary	late summer or autumn
Chamaecyparis lawsoniana (Lawson cypress)	formal evergreen	foliage	shelter	midsummer and/or autumn
Crataegus monogyna (hawthorn)	informal deciduous	flowers, fruit	wildlife	winter or early spring
x *Cupressocyparis leylandii* (Leyland cypress)	formal evergreen	foliage	shelter	midsummer and/or autumn
Elaeagnus x ebbingei	formal evergreen	foliage	shelter	late summer
Escallonia rubra	formal evergreen	foliage, flowers	shelter	midsummer and/or autumn
Fuchsia magellanica	informal deciduous	flowers	boundary	spring
Griselinia littoralis	formal evergreen	foliage	shelter	spring
Ilex aquifolium (holly)	formal/informal evergreen	foliage, berries	wildlife	late summer or early spring
Lavandula (lavender)	formal/informal evergreen	foliage, flowers	edging	spring and late summer
Ligustrum ovalifolium	informal evergreen	flowers	boundary	midsummer and/or autumn
Lonicera nitida (shrubby honeysuckle)	formal evergreen	foliage	edging	late spring, midsummer and autumn
Prunus laurocerasus (cherry laurel)	formal evergreen	foliage	shelter	late summer and autumn
Rosa rugosa (rose)	informal deciduous	flowers , fruit	boundary	late winter or early spring
Taxus baccata (yew)	formal evergreen	flowers, berries	boundary	late summer or autumn
Thuja plicata	formal evergreen	flowers	shelter	late summer or autumn
Viburnum tinus	formal/informal evergreen	flowers	boundary	late summer or autumn

Hedge shapes

Hedges can be clipped into different shapes, usually with the base wider than the top to protect them against the effects of wind and snow. You can also choose a flat, angled, or rounded top, depending on your preference.

Formal tapering hornbeam hedge This shape gives greater strength against wind damage and prevents snow from collecting on the top and breaking the stems.

Formal rounded conifer hedge A rounded top has a strong structure that reduces the likelihood of wind and snow damage. It also has a gentler, less formal appearance.

Formal tapering yew hedge This distinct, formally shaped hedge can only be achieved using plants with a very dense growth habit, such as yew, box, privet, or shrubby *Lonicera*.

Trimming a flat top Use shears to cut the top of a formal hedge to give a flat surface. Ensure the blades are horizontal so the cut is level – you may need to use a line to help you.

Using guides and lines To create a straight, level top, tie a length of string between two posts and pull taut to the height at which you want the hedge (*see also p.104*).

Angling trimmer to round edges For an informally shaped hedge, gently round the corners and edges with a trimmer. An informal hedge holds its shape well and is resistant to damage.

Leafy arch This archway has been made by training the hedging plants around a strong wooden or metal framework. The arch is cut more frequently than the sides to prevent it from closing up as the hedge grows.

How to prune a yew hedge

Yew (*Taxus*) is a versatile conifer that forms a dense hedge and can be trained to any height or shape. It is also one of the few conifers that will flourish after being hard pruned.

Tip for success

Use a tripod safety ladder when cutting a hedge above head height. Never over-stretch or lean out too far to either side.

1 A yew hedge will put on about 30cm (12in) of growth each year, and should be pruned in late summer to keep it within bounds. For a tall hedge you will need a safety ladder or platform to cut the top (*see facing page*).

2 Use a petrol or electric hedge cutter to trim the sides and top, cutting back to the previous summer's growth. Try to keep a straight edge as you work. Always wear safety eye protection and ear defenders when using a hedge cutter.

3 Standing on a safety ladder or platform and using a guideline (*see p.104*), cut the top of the hedge. Trim back to where the hedge was pruned last year. Work from one side, cutting half way across, and then the other.

Pruning a box hedge

For a formal effect, use box (*Buxus sempervirens*) hedging to edge paths and flowerbeds. Keep this compact evergreen looking tidy and to size by trimming in early summer.

1 Due to the young growth produced during the spring, this box hedge has lost its sharp, clipped appearance. Use shears for its annual haircut in summer – don't leave it too late as the foliage needs to harden off before winter.

2 Trim back the top of the hedge to the point where the new growths meet the old growths. You can recognise the young stems because they are much lighter in colour. Try to trim to the same level all the way along the top.

3 Cut the sides of the hedge in the same way as the top, trimming back to where the new growths have been produced. If in doubt about how much to cut off, trim in stages, cutting cautiously at first.

4 When you think you have finished, take a close look all over the hedge again. There are likely to be a few shoots that you will have missed, especially at the base and corners, so trim these off for an immaculate finish.

How to prune a beech hedge

After trimming, this beech hedge has a formal straight top and sides. Prune deciduous hedges in late summer so you do not disturb wildlife, such as birds, which may use them as nesting sites.

Tip for success

Beech hedges retain their brown dead leaves during the winter, providing seasonal texture and colour, so don't prune these out.

1 Use an electric or petrol hedge trimmer to cut your hedge. If using an electric trimmer, always ensure that the cable is behind you when you are cutting and the electricity supply is connected to an emergency circuit breaker.

2 Wearing goggles, cut one side of the hedge. Using a sweeping motion, work from the bottom to the top. Try to keep to the natural line of the hedge, reducing the width as required. Then trim the other side.

3 Work along the top of the hedge in a straight line, or create a rounded top if heavy snow is common in your area. Reduce the height by the amount you require, and use a guideline if needed (see p.104).

Renovating a hornbeam hedge

When a hornbeam (*Carpinus*) or beech (*Fagus*) hedge gets too big and holes appear, renovate it in late winter. This is a two-year process: cut one side one year and the other the next year.

1 This hornbeam hedge is over 40 years old and is becoming difficult to cut because it has grown so big. The aim of the renovation is to reduce its height and width by 90cm (36in), pruning one side first and then the top.

2 When pruning a hedge, always remove dead and diseased branches first. These are normally obvious in their appearance and must be cut back into healthy wood.

3 Use loppers to prune side branches that are difficult to reach or awkwardly placed. These branches are likely to be too thick for secateurs, which should not be used on stems any thicker than 1.5cm (½in) in diameter.

Renovating a hornbeam hedge *continued*

4 When removing branches that are above head height, always wear eye protection to prevent sawdust and debris getting into your eyes. A pruning saw is easier than loppers to use at this height.

5 To create a horizontal top, attach string to two posts secured at either end of the hedge, and keep the string taut. To check that the hedge is level across its width, place another cane horizontally on top of the string.

6 Use a tripod or platform-style ladder to access the top of the hedge. If your hedge is very long, you may find it easier to erect canes and horizontal guidelines across a part of it, and move them as you work along the hedge.

7 Use a pruning saw to cut thick branches at the top of the hedge. Start with those closest to you. If the hedge is very wide, you may have to move to the other side of it to cut the branches furthest away from you.

8 To give the hedge time to regenerate and build up its strength only cut one side and the top in the first year. Cut the other side the following year. The hedge may look skeletal, but it will soon spring back to life.

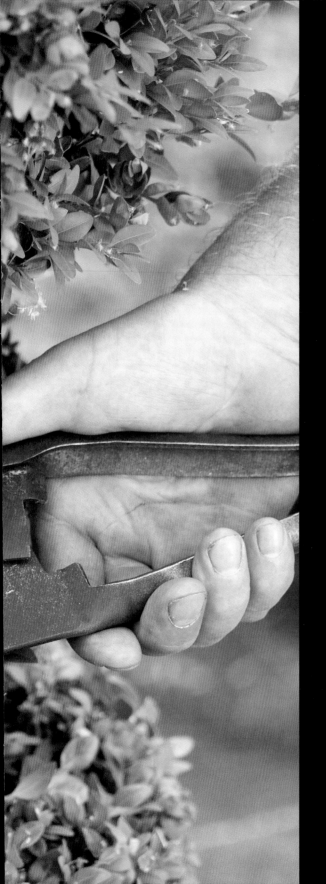

Training and shaping

Pruning to achieve special effects is a skill, but with a little practice you can create some wonderful features for your garden and patio. Roses wound round rope swags make beautiful walkways or screens, while an elegant spiral topiary will provide a stunning focal point on a patio or in a border. You will need a few specialist tools to make and maintain your features, but they represent good value when compared to the price of a finished piece of topiary at a garden centre. The basic topiary methods are outlined in this chapter, and can be used as a starting point from which to make whatever shapes inspire you.

Training a rose on a rope

Climbing and rambling roses can be easily trained along rope swags to make flowering screens or scented walkways. Here, the ropes are hidden beneath the dainty white blooms of *Rosa mulliganii*.

When to prune

In late autumn, the rose stems are very pliable and easy to prune and train without damaging them.

1 Remove the stems from the ropes, cutting out any dead, diseased, and damaged growths as you go. Be careful not to damage any of the strong, young growths produced from the base of the plant – they will be needed later.

2 Cut out one in three of the oldest stems at the base. It may be necessary to use a pruning saw or loppers as these growths can be thick. Also remove any dead wood at the base as this could harbour infection.

3 Spur prune last season's flowering side shoots that are attached to the remaining older stems (*see pp.34–35*). Tie these pruned stems and younger growths shooting up from the base of the plant back on to the support.

4 When the stems have been tied to the support, start attaching them to the rope swags. Try to allot an equal number of stems to each swag. You may find it helpful to wind the stems around the rope and then tie them in.

Making a standard plant

A plant trained with a long, clean stem and round bushy head is called a "standard". Fuchsia, box, viburnum and holly, as used here, all make wonderful standard plants.

1 This holly (*Ilex* x *altaclarensis* 'Golden King') has no clear stem or definite head, but these features are easy to create with a little pruning. First, decide the height at which you want the head to develop.

2 Remove some of the lowest side branches from the main stem, but don't be tempted to remove them all in one go, as they help to pull sap up the plant. Only once you have a decent round head on the plant can you remove them all.

3 To create a bushy head, shorten leggy growths by 5–15cm (2–6in), pruning above a leaf bud, and pinch out the soft tips of the shorter stems. Both methods encourage shoots to grow from many of the buds below the cuts.

4 Insert a cane or strong stake to support the main stem, which will still be quite weak at this early stage of training. Tie the main stem securely to the stake. Trim the head to shape each year and it will gradually fill out.

Topiary tools and techniques

With just a few tools and some simple pruning techniques you can create your own beautiful, inexpensive topiary. Use small-leaved plants, such as box (*Buxus*), conifers, and shrubby honeysuckle (*Lonicera nitida*), for the best effects.

Choosing tools and plants The most common plant used for topiary is box (*Buxus*) because it is easy to grow, thriving in sun or shade, and has dense evergreen leaves ideal for clipping into ornamental shapes. Buy a specimen with a good, even shape and either plant it in the garden in well prepared soil or in a container filled with soil-based compost, such as John Innes No 2. You will also need a pair of secateurs, topiary shears (*right*), and a pair of long-handled shears to create your plant sculptures.

Using topiary tools

When creating a topiary shape you may first need to remove long wayward stems with secateurs. Topiary shears (*above right*) are useful for clipping small balls and more intricate shapes, such as spirals (*see p.116–7*), while long-handled shears (*below*) are ideal for cones and simple shapes. Cranked topiary and long-handled shears are slightly angled, allowing you to follow the contours of a curved shape, such as a cone. Use the shears curved side down to clip the top of the cone (*below left*) and then flip them over to trim the bottom (*below right*).

Homemade templates You can buy topiary templates in a wide range of shapes, or create your own from garden wire. A useful trick for a circular template is to cut off a length of wire from a reel and twist the ends together.

Sterilizing tools To prevent the spread of disease, clean your tools with a sterilizing solution before trimming a new plant. Inexpensive household disinfectant will do the job, but also rub on some oil after use to prevent rust.

Using canes

Some topiary experts use canes as guides for straight-sided shapes, while others find it easier to work by eye. Canes are also useful for training plants to stand upright. For example, the peacock below is leaning slightly to the right. To rectify this problem, a long cane has been inserted into the ground about 30cm (12in) behind the topiary and at an angle of about 60°, leaning into it (*below left*). The head of the bird has then been pushed behind the cane to straighten it up. After a few months, the cane can be removed and the bird will be vertical.

Creating a topiary cone

Simple, architectural topiary shapes, such as cones, suit many situations, adding structure to formal borders and elegant terraces. They are also very easy to create.

1 When buying box or other topiary plants, look for healthy specimens densely covered in unblemished leaves, with a strong leading upright shoot in the centre. Before planting, ensure that its "best" side is facing the front.

2 Stand above the plant, and locate a central shoot that will form the point at the top of the cone. With long-handled shears, start to trim the box from this point in an outward direction. Keep moving around the plant as you clip.

3 Stand back from time to time to assess the shape of the cone. To achieve a perfectly circular cone, look directly down at it from the central point. From this position you can see if the cone is clipped equally all around.

4 If your cone has a few gaps, don't be tempted to keep trimming, or you will end up with a tiny topiary. Leave the gaps, and after a few months young shoots will form and fill them out. Tidy up your cone twice a year in summer.

Making a spiral topiary

To create this sculptural spiral with a lollipop top, use a rounded shrub, and clip the lower two-thirds into a cone (*see pp.114–5*). Then follow these steps to finish it off.

Tip for success

To make a globe, use a circular template made from a reel of wire (*see p.113*). Leave any gaps to grow out and fill the spaces.

1 When you have created a cone with the lower two-thirds of the plant, roughly shape the ball on top with a pair of topiary shears. Ensure that your lollipop looks in proportion with the cone – not too big or too small.

2 Begin shaping the spiral with topiary shears. Clip into the centre stem of the plant, about 20cm (8in) or more from the bottom, to create an upward-sloping indentation. Move around the plant, clipping into it at the same angle.

3 The spiral should be slightly deeper at the bottom of the plant and narrow towards the top. Take your time and stand back now and again to check your work. Round off the edges of the spiral to form a sausage shape.

4 Finish off the spiral and then shape the lollipop top. Clip a little at a time with topiary shears, using a template to guide you (*see left*). Keep stepping back and check with your template that the lollipop is spherical from all angles.

Plant pruning guide

This indispensable guide outlines the pruning requirements of a wide range of popular garden plants, detailing how and when to make your cuts. The symbols below indicate the growing conditions that each of the plants prefers.

Key to plant symbols

ᵂ Plants given the RHS Award of Garden Merit

Soil preference

◊ Well-drained soil

◊ Moist soil

● Wet soil

Preference for sun or shade

☼ Full sun

☼ Partial or dappled shade

☀ Full shade

Hardiness ratings

✳✳✳ Fully hardy plants

✳✳ Plants that survive outside in mild regions or sheltered sites

✳ Plants that need protection from frost over winter

❀ Tender plants that do not tolerate any degree of frost

Plant pruning guide (Ab–Ca)

Abelia x grandiflora

This *Abelia* is grown for its flowers or attractive variegated or gold foliage. In spring, prune out any stems with leaves that have lost their variegation. Usually requires little pruning except for leggy branches, and dead or damaged stems.

H: 3m (10ft); **S**: 4m (12ft)
❄❄ ◊ ☼ ♉

Acer davidii

The snake-bark maple is famed for its beautiful bark, which provides wonderful winter interest. It is best grown on a single, clear trunk, which is achieved when the plant is small by removing all the lower branches in summer or winter with secateurs.

H: 15m (50ft); **S**: 15m (50ft)
❄❄❄ ◊ ☼ ☀

Acer palmatum

All cultivars are grown for their lovely foliage and autumn colours. Prune leggy branches in midsummer to maintain a good shape. Remove any winter die-back in early spring and dead, diseased, or damaged branches when you see them.

H: 8m (25ft); **S**: 10m (30ft)
❄❄❄ ◊ ☼ ☀

Actinidia deliciosa

Kiwi fruit is a climber grown for its lovely foliage and autumn colours. Prune leggy branches in midsummer to maintain a good shape. Remove any winter die-back in early spring and dead, diseased, or damaged branches when you see them.

H: 10m (30ft)
❄❄ ◊ ☼ ☀

Artemisia 'Powis Castle'

This feathery shrub has attractive silver foliage that is lightly trimmed in spring to maintain its shape and to encourage growth. Give it a light shear as for lavender (see *pp.64–65*), but do not cut it back too hard or the plant will not rejuvenate.

H: 60cm (24in); **S**: 90cm (36in)
❄❄ ◊ ☼ ♉

Aucuba japonica

Grown for its glossy evergreen leaves, female plants can also bear attractive red berries, and many cultivars have decoratively spotted or variegated foliage. Prune plants lightly at any time to keep their shape; they also respond well to hard pruning.

H: 3m (10ft); **S**: 3m (10ft)
❄❄❄ ◊ ◗ ☼ ◑ ☀

Berberis x stenophylla
Grow this prickly gold-flowered plant as a freestanding shrub or hedge. If it gets too big, prune as for a mahonia (*see pp.68–69*). To keep compact, after flowering remove one-third of the oldest stems and shorten leggy stems. Wear thick gloves.

H: 3m (10ft); **S**: 5m (15ft)
❄❄❄ ◌ ◑ ☼ ◐ ☉

Berberis thunbergii
Compact, with yellow flowers, bright red berries and great autumn colour, this berberis has many uses. Wearing thick gloves, lightly prune in late summer or early autumn to maintain its shape, or prune like a mahonia (*see pp.68–69*) if it becomes too big.

H: 1m (3ft); **S**: 2.5m (8ft)
❄❄❄ ◌ ◑ ☼ ◐ ☉

Betula utilis *var.* jacquemontii
Grown for its attractive silvery-white bark, remove the lower branches over several years as it matures. A trunk of 2m (6ft) is ideal for showing off the bark. Also remove any damaged, diseased, or crossing branches from the canopy in midsummer or winter.

H: 18m (60ft); **S**: 10m (30ft)
❄❄❄ ◌ ◑ ☼ ◐

Buddleja davidii
The butterfly bush is a vigorous summer-flowering shrub. Prune it in late winter or early spring. Cut the branches back to two buds from the base of last season's growth. After flowering, also remove spent flowers to prevent them seeding.

H: 3m (10ft); **S**: 5m (15ft)
❄❄❄ ◌ ◑ ☼ ◐

Buxus sempervirens
Often used as a small, formal hedge, this evergreen can also be trained into topiary shapes. When trained in either way, it is advisable to prune at least twice a year: once in late spring, and then again in midsummer.

H: 5m (15ft); **S**: 5m (15ft)
❄❄❄ ◌ ◑ ☼ ◐ ☉

Calluna vulgaris
Common Scottish heather flowers during the summer months, and some cultivars have lovely golden foliage. For best results, it should be trimmed annually with shears in early spring, but don't cut back into old wood as the plant will not rejuvenate.

H: 10–60cm (4–24in); **S**: up to 75cm (30in) ❄❄❄ ◌ ☼

Plant pruning guide (Ca–Ch)

Camellia japonica
This evergreen spring-flowering shrub does not require much pruning. To maintain its shape, branches may need trimming back after flowering. If the plant has grown too large, reduce and rejuvenate it by very hard pruning (*see pp.54–55*) in summer.

H: 9m (28ft); **S**: 8m (25ft)
❀❀❀ ◐ ☼ ☀

Camellia x williamsii 'Donation'
A spring-flowering evergreen shrub that is grown as a specimen plant or informal hedge. Remove leggy growths after flowering to maintain the plant's health. If it has grown too large, hard prune to rejuvenate after flowering (*see pp.54–55*).

H: 5m (15ft); **S**: 2.5m (8ft)
❀❀❀ ◐ ☼ ☀ ♚

Campsis x tagliabuana
Train this vigorous exotic-looking climber, which flowers in the summer, up a wall, fence, or other permanent structure. To keep the plant at a manageable size, spur prune each of the stems back to two pairs of buds in early spring (*see pp.34–35*).

H: 10m (30ft)
❀❀ ◐ ◐ ☼ ☀

Carpinus betulus
Hornbeam is a deciduous tree that can be used as either a freestanding ornamental plant or hedging. When grown as a tree, minimal pruning is required, but trim a hedge in late summer, or renovate old hedges in late winter (*see pp.102–105*).

H: 25m (80ft); **S**: 20m (70ft)
❀❀❀ ◐ ◐ ☼ ☀ ♚

Caryopteris x clandonensis 'Arthur Simmonds'
This lovely small shrub has beautiful blue flowers in late summer and decorative, aromatic silver foliage. Prune it lightly in early spring, as for *Fuchsia magellanica* (*see p.129*).

H: 1m (3ft); **S**: 1.5m (5ft)
❀❀❀ ◐ ☼ ♚

Catalpa bignonioides
When grown as a tree, prune only to remove dead, diseased, and crossing stems. Alternatively, coppice young plants annually (*see pp.36–37*), to contain their size and encourage strong growths with extra large, decorative leaves.

H: 15m (50ft); **S**: 15m (50ft)
❀❀❀ ◐ ☼ ♚

Ceanothus 'Blue Mound'
This form of the evergreen California lilac flowers in early summer. A light pruning after flowering helps to maintain the size of the *Ceanothus* (*see p.56*), but do not cut hard back into the old wood as plants don't normally regenerate.

H: 1.5m (5ft); **S**: 2m (6ft)
❋❋ ◊ ◐ ☼ ◑ ♈

Ceratostigma willmottianum
This wonderful little shrub has lovely blue flowers in the late summer. To prune, cut all the previous year's growths down to just above ground level in early to mid-spring. Mulch with garden compost and the plant will erupt into growth.

H: 1m (3ft); **S**: 1.5m (5ft)
❋❋❋ ◊ ◐ ☼ ♈

Cercis canadensis 'Forest Pansy'
A small tree that is grown for its early summer lilac-pink flowers and purple foliage, which turns vibrant red in the autumn. Prune carefully when young to create a good branch structure. Thereafter, prune only if it becomes too large or branches get in the way.

H: 10m (30ft); **S**: 10m (30ft)
❋❋❋ ◊ ◐ ☼ ◑ ♈

Chaenomeles *cultivars*
Grow flowering quinces as free-standing shrubs or train against a wall. Prune after flowering, cutting all new growths back to five or six buds. These will produce spurs covered in flowers the following spring. Also remove long or wayward branches.

H: up to 2.5m (8ft); **S**: up to 3m (10ft)
❋❋❋ ◊ ☼ ◑

Chimonanthus praecox
A highly scented, winter-flowering shrub whose flowers are produced from stems that are several years old, so prune just the leggy growths after flowering has finished. If it is too large, hard prune in the winter, but it then will not flower for several years.

H: 4m (12ft); **S**: 3m (10ft)
❋❋❋ ◊ ☼

Choisya ternata
The Mexican orange blossom is a flowering evergreen shrub. It requires little pruning, apart from removing in spring growths damaged by winter frosts. If the plant is looking untidy, it responds very well to hard pruning almost to ground level in early spring.

H: 2.5m (8ft); **S**: 2.5m (8ft)
❋❋❋ ◊ ◐ ☼ ♈

Plant pruning guide (Cl–Co)

Clematis alpina

Violet-blue flowers appear in spring on last year's growth, followed by attractive fluffy seedheads. To prune, remove dead or damaged growths in early spring. For an overgrown plant, hard prune to 15cm (6in) from the ground in early spring (*see p.81*).

H: 2–3m (6–10ft), Group 1
❋❋❋ ◊ ◊ ☼ ◐ ☽ ♈

Clematis armandii

This evergreen clematis has large white, scented flowers. It is not fully hardy and prefers the shelter of a warm, sunny wall or fence. To prune, remove any growths in spring that have died or been damaged by cold winter weather (*see p.81*).

H: 3–5m (10–15ft), Group 1
❋❋ ◊ ◊ ☼ ◐

Clematis 'Etoile Violette'

A vigorous clematis that produces masses of purple flowers in late summer on its current year's growth. To prune, cut back all growths to 15–30cm (6–12in) above ground level in early spring (*see pp.82–83*).

H: 3–5m (10–15ft), Group 3
❋❋❋ ◊ ◊ ☼ ◐ ☽ ♈

Clematis 'H.F. Young'

This clematis has large blue flowers in early summer. Prune lightly in early spring. Working from the top, prune each stem to the first pair of healthy buds. If the plant becomes too large, hard prune in early spring to 15cm (6in) above ground level (*see p.81*).

H: 2.5m (8ft), Group 2
❋❋❋ ◊ ◊ ☼ ◐

Clematis 'Jackmanii'

Producing masses of deep purple-blue flowers in summer on its current year's stems, this old favourite should be pruned in early spring. Cut back all growth to 15–30cm (6–12in) above ground level (*see pp.82–83*).

H: 3m (10ft), Group 3
❋❋❋ ◊ ◊ ☼ ◐ ☽ ♈

Clematis 'Nelly Moser'

This popular clematis produces large pink flowers in late spring and again in late summer. Prune lightly in early spring, cutting each stem back to the first pair of healthy buds. Hard prune overgrown plants to 15cm (6in) from the ground (*see p.81*) in early spring.

H: 2–3m (6–10ft), Group 2
❋❋❋ ◊ ◊ ☼ ◐ ☽ ♈

Cornus alba

Dogwood is grown for its lovely winter stem colours and, of the many varieties, *C. alba* is a cheerful red. To encourage strong, colourful stems, prune in spring (*see pp.36–37*). If left unpruned, the stems start to loose their winter colours with age.

H: 3m (10ft); **S**: 3m (10ft)
❄❄❄ ◊ ◊ ◖ ☼ ◑

Cornus alternifolia '*Variegata*'

This lovely shrub has white flowers in spring and variegated leaves cover its tiered branches. To prune, remove lower branches of young plants for a more distinct shape, and occasionally thin the canopies of older trees to emphasize their horizontal structure.

H: 3m (10ft); **S**: 2.5m (8ft)
❄❄❄ ◊ ◊ ☼ ◑

Cornus kousa *var.* chinensis

The white bracts in late spring, red summer fruits and autumn leaves make this a valuable garden plant. In summer or winter, remove some lower branches on young plants so you can see the ornamental bark, and cut out crossing stems in the canopy.

H: 7m (22ft); **S**: 5m (15ft)
❄❄❄ ◊ ◊ ☼ ◑ ♔

Cornus sanguinea '*Winter Beauty*'

To produce wonderful multicoloured stems during the winter, prune this pretty dogwood in late spring to encourage strong growths. When young, it is advisable not to prune it for two years to help it to establish; you can then prune annually.

H: 3m (10ft); **S**: 2.5m (8ft)
❄❄❄ ◊ ◊ ◖ ☼ ◑

Corylus avellana '*Contorta*'

A slow-growing shrub with contorted stems, this hazel looks its best during the winter. In spring and summer, the branches are hidden under a mass of untidy leaves. Prune it only to remove any damaged, diseased, dead, or crossing branches.

H: 5m (15ft); **S**: 5m (15ft)
❄❄❄ ◊ ◊ ☼ ◑

Cotinus coggygria

The smoke bush is grown for its colourful foliage and plume-like flowers. If left unpruned, it can become very large, so trim annually, but you may lose the flowers. For strong growth with larger leaves, hard prune annually (*see pp.48–49*).

H: 5m (15ft); **S**: 5m (15ft)
❄❄❄ ◊ ◊ ☼ ◑ ♔

Plant pruning guide (Co–Eu)

Cotoneaster horizontalis

This low-growing shrub is excellent for covering walls and banks, and it is also suitable as ground cover. *Cotoneaster* has wonderful red berries in the autumn. Prune in early spring to retain its shape and to prevent it from spreading too far.

H: 1m (3ft); **S**: 1.5m (5ft)
❄❄❄ ◊ ◐ ☼ ☀ ♈

Crataegus monogyna

The hawthorn is widely grown as an ornamental tree or as a hedging plant. It has scented flowers in late spring and is covered in red berries in autumn. No pruning is required for a tree but trim a hedge in early spring to reduce any wildlife disturbance.

H: 10m (30ft); **S**: 8m (25ft)
❄❄❄ ◊ ◐ ☼ ☀

Cytisus x praecox

This flowering broom is covered with golden yellow flowers in early summer. It requires minimal pruning, but can be given a light trim immediately after flowering to retain its shape. Do not cut back into the old wood as it will not regenerate.

H: 1.2m (4ft); **S**: 1.5m (5ft)
❄❄❄ ◊ ☼

Daboecia cantabrica f. alba

Give summer-flowering members of the heather family a light trim with a pair of shears in early spring. Remove all the old flowers but don't be tempted to cut into the old wood as this plant will not rejuvenate.

H: 25–40cm (10–16in); **S**: 65cm (26in) ❄❄❄ ◊ ☼ ☀

Daphne bholua

The sweetly scented flowers of this shrub appear in winter. Pinch out the growing tips of young plants to encourage a bushy habit (*see pp.42–43*). This can also be done to older specimens, but do not hard prune as the plant will not respond well.

H: 2–4m (6–12ft); **S**: 1.5m (5ft)
❄❄ ◊ ☼ ☀

Deutzia x hybrida 'Mont Rose'

This lovely early summer-flowering shrub is easy to grow. Prune after flowering as for *Philadelphus* (*see p.57*), and aim to remove about one-third of the old stems to encourage new growths to push through from the base of the plant.

H: 1.2m (4ft); **S**: 1.2m (4ft)
❄❄❄ ◊ ◐ ☼ ☀ ♈

Elaeagnus pungens 'Maculata'
This evergreen with gold-splashed foliage is grown as a freestanding shrub or a hedge. Prune in winter or spring by cutting back the previous season's growth to two or three leaf buds. To avoid reversion, cut back all-green leaves to golden foliage.

H: 4m (12ft); **S**: 5m (15ft)
❄❄❄ ◊ ☀

Erica arborea var. alpina
The heather family includes many varieties, and this is one of the larger members. Tree heath produces masses of scented white flowers in the spring. Unlike other heathers, overgrown plants respond very well to hard pruning in mid-spring.

H: 2m (6ft); **S**: 85cm (34in)
❄❄❄ ◊ ☀ ⚱

Erica carnea
This pretty winter-flowering member of the heather family should be pruned with shears in mid- to late spring. Remove the flowers but do not cut into the old wood, as the plant will not regenerate (see p.41).

H: 20–25cm (8–10); **S**: 55cm (22in)
❄❄❄ ◊ ☀

Erica cinerea f. alba
The bell heather flowers from mid- to late summer. Trim in early spring using shears to remove the old flower spikes. Don't cut into old wood as the plant will not regenerate (see p.41).

H: 30cm (12in); **S**: 55cm (22in)
❄❄❄ ◊ ☀

Escallonia 'Apple Blossom'
Grow this evergreen, early summer-flowering shrub as a hedge or a freestanding plant. From mid- to late summer, cut back flowering shoots by one-half to keep the plant relatively compact. For plants that are too large, hard prune after flowering.

H: 2.5m (8ft); **S**: 2.5m (8ft)
❄❄❄ ◊ ◑ ☀ ⚱

Eucalyptus gunnii
This beautiful plant has distinctive silver-blue foliage. It can be allowed to grow into a large tree but to keep it as a small bush, hard prune annually in early spring. The resulting vibrantly coloured young foliage also makes an excellent focal point.

H: to 25m (80ft); **S**: to 15m (50ft)
❄❄ ◊ ◑ ☀ ⚱

Plant pruning guide (Eu–Ha)

Euonymus europaeus
The spindle tree is grown for its autumn colours and interesting fruits. Prune young trees to create a good shape and structure; older trees require little pruning apart from the removal of dead, damaged, or diseased wood, and crossing stems.

H: 3m (10ft); **S**: 2.5m (8ft)
❄❄❄ ◊ ◗ ☼ ☀

Euonymus fortunei
Train this evergreen foliage plant up a wall or fence, or grow it as ground cover or a freestanding shrub. Lightly trim in early spring to maintain a good shape. Remove immediately any reversion (stems with all-green foliage) on variegated forms.

H: 60cm (24in); **S**: indefinite
❄❄❄ ◊ ◗ ☼ ☀

Exochorda x macrantha 'The Bride'
This late spring-flowering shrub has masses of white flowers that hang from its long branches. To maintain a young, vigorous plant, remove some of the oldest stems each spring. Hard prune an overgrown plant in spring, but you will lose a year's flowering.

H: 2m (6ft); **S**: 3m (10ft)
❄❄❄ ◊ ◗ ☼ ☀ ♀

x Fatshedera lizei
This evergreen shrub has large, shiny leaves similar in shape to ivy, and is suitable for shady areas. It is an excellent foliage plant and requires very little pruning apart from removing leggy growths. This is best done in the spring.

H: 1.2–2m (4–6ft); **S**: 3m (10ft)
❄❄ ◊ ◗ ☼ ☀

Forsythia x intermedia 'Lynwood Variety'
The vivid yellow spring flowers of this large shrub appear on the previous season's branches. After flowering, remove annually one in three of the oldest branches. Hard prune overgrown plants in early spring.

H: 3m (10ft); **S**: 3m (10ft)
❄❄❄ ◊ ◗ ☼ ☀ ♀

Fremontodendron 'California Glory'
This evergreen shrub is normally grown against a sunny wall. Occasionally, very long growths may need to be reduced in length in early summer. Be careful when pruning as the plant can cause skin irritation.

H: 6m (20ft); **S**: 4m (12ft)
❄❄ ◊ ☼ ♀

Fuchsia magellanica

An elegant summer-flowering plant, this fuchsia is grown as a freestanding shrub or a flowering hedge. In early spring, lightly trim the plant just back into green, healthy stems. After a severe winter, however, prune back to ground level.

H: 3m (10ft); **S**: 2–3m (6–10ft)
❄❄ ◊ ◑ ☼ ◐

Garrya elliptica 'James Roof'

A large, slightly tender, evergreen shrub normally grown against a sunny wall for winter protection. It is covered in long, decorative catkins in late winter, which provide an exciting feature. Prune annually in early spring to contain its size (see p67).

H: 4m (12ft); **S**: 4m (12ft)
❄❄ ◊ ☼ ◐ ♈

Gaultheria mucronata

A dwarf evergreen, suckering shrub, *Gaultheria* is covered with very showy, wax-like fruits during the autumn. Minimal pruning is required unless the plant is spreading too much and needs to be contained. This is best done in early spring.

H: 1.2m (4ft); **S**: 1.2m (4ft)
❄❄❄ ◑ ☼ ◐

Genista aetnensis

The Mount Etna broom is a large, graceful shrub with scented summer flowers. To keep it in shape and encourage flowering growths, prune lightly immediately after flowering. Do not cut back into old wood as the shrub will not regenerate.

H: 8m (25ft); **S**: 8m (25ft)
❄❄❄ ◊ ☼ ♈

Griselinia littoralis

This is an excellent evergreen that can be grown as a specimen shrub or a hedge. Trim hedges in late summer and freestanding shrubs in early spring if they become too large. Remove growths damaged by cold, frosty weather in early spring.

H: 8m (25ft); **S**: 5m (15ft)
❄❄❄ ◊ ☼ ♈

Hamamelis x intermedia 'Pallida'

Hamamelis is a wonderful, scented late winter- or early spring-flowering shrub. It is suitable for a small garden if it is contained in size. To do this, spur prune all the previous year's growths to two or three buds once flowering has finished (see pp.50–51).

H: 4m (12ft); **S**: 4m (12ft)
❄❄❄ ◊ ◑ ☼ ◐ ♈

Plant pruning guide (He–Ja)

Hedera helix
Ivies are very versatile, self-clinging climbers. They will cover walls, fences, and trees, and also make good ground cover. When too large, prune back hard in spring to reduce the size. Trim at any time from late spring to midsummer to keep neat.

H: 10m (30ft)
❋❋❋ ◊ ◊ ◆ ☼ ☀

Hydrangea arborescens
'Grandiflora'
This summer-flowering hydrangea has large, creamy-white flowerheads. It flowers on new growth and can be pruned like a perennial plant, cutting back to 5–10cm (2–4in) above ground level in early spring.

H: 2.5m (8ft); **S**: 2.5m (8ft)
❋❋❋ ◊ ◊ ☼ ☀ ♈

Hydrangea macrophylla
Mophead hydrangea flowerheads are produced on the previous season's growth. Leave them on the plant over winter to give frost protection. In mid-spring, cut back last year's growth to a pair of healthy buds and remove weak or dead shoots (*see p.47*).

H: 2m (6ft); **S**: 2.5m (8ft)
❋❋❋ ◊ ◊ ☼ ☀

Hydrangea paniculata
These hydrangeas produce large cone-shaped flowerheads on the current season's growth. To keep them small, prune all the previous season's stems back in early spring to two or three pairs of buds to leave a low structure of stems (*see p.46*).

H: 3–7m (10–22ft); **S**: 2.5m (8ft)
❋❋❋ ◊ ◊ ☼ ☀

Hydrangea petiolaris
This self-clinging, climbing hydrangea requires little pruning. Remove growths that are too long in early spring, and old flowerheads after flowering. If the plant is too vigorous, prune hard in early spring, but it may then not flower for up to two years.

H: 15m (50ft)
❋❋❋ ◊ ◊ ☼ ☀

Hypericum 'Hidcote'
To keep this plant compact and producing masses of yellow summer flowers, remove dead or diseased wood in early spring and prune the remaining stems to 5–10cm (2–4in) from the ground. Also cut out one-third of older stems on large shrubs.

H: 1.2m (4ft); **S**: 1.5m (5ft)
❋❋❋ ◊ ◊ ☼ ☀ ♈

Ilex aquifolium 'Pyramidalis Aureomarginata'

This holly makes a bold, freestanding tree (see pp.70–71). It can also be trained into a formal shape or used as a hedge. Prune in early spring (all hollies tolerate severe pruning) and remove all-green foliage on sight.

H: 6m (20ft); **S**: 5m (15ft)
❀❀❀ ◊ ◖ ☼ ☀

Ilex crenata

Box-leaved holly has small leaves and glossy black berries and makes an excellent clipped hedge or topiary plant. It is a suitable alternative to a box hedge (Buxus) and is trimmed in the same way (see pp.98–99).

H: 5m (15ft); **S**: 4m (12ft)
❀❀❀ ◊ ◖ ☼ ☀

Indigofera heterantha

This flowering shrub is covered with masses of pink, pea-like flowers during the summer. Hard prune large plants in early spring. In severe winters it may suffer from die-back, but if hard pruned, it will produce a mass of shoots from low down.

H: 2–3m (6–10ft); **S**: 2–3m (6–10ft)
❀❀❀ ◊ ◖ ☼ ♈

Itea ilicifolia

This evergreen shrub has masses of finger-like stems of green flowers in the summer. It can be grown as a freestanding shrub or against a wall. When young, prune and pinch the plant to shape it in early spring. When older, just trim long growths .

H: 3–5m (10–15ft); **S**: 3m (10ft)
❀❀ ◊ ◖ ☼ ♈

Jasminum nudiflorum

The winter jasmine produces bright yellow flowers over a long period throughout winter and early spring. It is normally trained against a wall or fence. Prune long, leggy growths immediately after it has finished flowering in early spring.

H: 3m (10ft); **S**: 3m (10ft)
❀❀❀ ◊ ◖ ☼ ☀ ♈

Jasminum officinale

Common jasmine has white, scented flowers in the summer. It is a vigorous climber and can be trained up walls or over other structures. Trim at any time to keep the plant within bounds. Hard prune plants that have grown too large in early spring.

H: 12m (40ft)
❀❀ ◊ ◖ ☼ ☀ ♈

Plant pruning guide (Ke–Lu)

Kerria japonica *'Golden Guinea'*

A clump-forming suckering shrub covered with large, golden flowers in late spring, *Kerria* can soon outgrow its situation. To contain its size, prune it hard or thin out old stems after flowering each year.

H: 2m (6ft); **S**: 2.5m (8ft)
❄❄❄ ◊ ◊ ☼ ☼ ☼ ♀

Kolkwitzia amabilis *'Pink Cloud'*

The beauty bush is a large shrub with pendulous branches covered in pink flowers in late spring. Prune it after flowering, removing about one-third of the old flowering stems (*see p.57*). Cut back large plants in early spring to 30cm (12in) above the ground.

H: 3m (10ft); **S**: 4m (12ft)
❄❄❄ ◊ ◊ ☼ ♀

Laurus nobilis

Bay laurel is an evergreen shrub that can be trained into many formal shapes and makes an excellent topiary specimen. Prune formal and topiary plants (*see pp.112–117*) during early summer, but use secateurs rather than shears to shape them.

H: 12m (40ft); **S**: 10m (30ft)
❄❄ ◊ ◊ ☼ ☼ ♀

Lavandula angustifolia

This lavender is a mass of blue-purple aromatic flowers during the summer. It makes an excellent low-growing hedge. For best results, prune twice a year: shear back in early spring and then trim lightly once it has finished flowering (*see pp.64–65*).

H: 1m (3ft); **S**: 1.2m (4ft)
❄❄❄ ◊ ☼

Lavatera x clementii *'Barnsley'*

Mallow is a shrubby perennial that produces an abundance of large, pale pink summer flowers. To keep a plant young and healthy, prune in spring to a framework of strong stems about 30cm (12in) high. Also remove any dead, diseased, or weak branches.

H: 2m (6ft); **S**: 2m (6ft)
❄❄❄ ◊ ☼

Lespedeza thunbergii

A lovely late summer-flowering shrubby perennial, bush clover has arching stems covered in deep pink, pea-like flowers. Prune back all the stems in spring to just above ground level and new young shoots will quickly appear.

H: 2m (6ft); **S**: 3m (10ft)
❄❄❄ ◊ ☼ ♀

Leycesteria formosa

This shrub has white flowers surrounded by maroon bracts during the summer, followed by purple berries. It is almost indestructible and can be left unpruned, or it grows just as well if it is hard pruned every year in early spring.

H: 2m (6ft); **S**: 2m (6ft)
❋❋❋ ◊ ◑ ☼ ☼ ☽ ♈

Ligustrum lucidum

The panicles of white flowers on this evergreen shrub appear during late summer. It has a lovely, even shape and requires minimal pruning. Occasionally, it may be necessary to trim a few of the branches to maintain its shape.

H: 10m (30ft); **S**: 10m (30ft)
❋❋❋ ◊ ☼ ☼ ☽ ♈

Lonicera nitida

This form of evergreen honeysuckle is often used as a hedging plant or a shrub. When grown as a hedge, trim it several times in the summer to maintain its shape. For a free-standing shrub, remove about a third of the older stems in early spring.

H: 3.5m (11ft); **S**: 3m (10ft)
❋❋❋ ◊ ◑ ☼ ☼

Lonicera periclymenum
'Graham Thomas'

If it's a highly scented summer-flowering climber that you are after, this is the plant for you. If it becomes straggly, prune in early spring. Also remove any dead or damaged wood at this time (*see p.84*).

H: 7m (22ft)
❋❋❋ ◊ ◑ ☼ ☽ ♈

Lonicera x purpusii

This shrubby honeysuckle is grown for its creamy white, highly scented winter flowers. To keep the plant to a manageable size, remove one-third of the old stems to almost ground level in early spring (*see p.52–53*).

H: 2m (6ft); **S**: 2.5m (8ft)
❋❋❋ ◊ ☼ ☽

Luma apiculata

An evergreen shrub or small tree grown for its attractive peeling bark and small white flowers, which appear in late summer. As it grows, remove some of the lower branches in summer so that you can fully appreciate the wonderful bark.

H: 10–15m (30–50ft); **S**: 10–15m (30–50ft) ❋❋❋ ◊ ☼ ☽ ♈

Plant pruning guide (Ma–Ph)

Magnolia grandiflora

Grow this lovely evergreen, summer-flowering tree against a south-facing wall, and prune in the spring or summer to maintain its shape. Pruning reduces the chance of die-back and allows the wounds to heal before the cold winter months set in.

H: 6–18m (20–60ft); **S**: 15m (50ft)
❄❄ ◊ ◖ ☼ ☀

Magnolia x loebneri 'Leonard Messel'

This spring-flowering tree requires minimal pruning. When it is young, you may need to remove a few lower branches in the spring or summer to give it a good shape. As it gets older, cut back any obstructive branches.

H: 8m (25ft); **S**: 6m (20ft)
❄❄❄ ◊ ◖ ☼ ☀ ♈ ▽

Mahonia aquifolium

An evergreen suckering shrub that flowers in the winter and makes good ground cover. To keep Oregon grape a reasonable size, cut it down to ground level every three or four years after flowering, or remove one-third of the oldest stems every year.

H: 1m (3ft); **S**: 1m (3ft)
❄❄❄ ◊ ◖ ☼ ☀ ☀

Mahonia x media 'Charity'

If this evergreen, winter-flowering shrub has outgrown its site, hard prune in early spring (see pp.68–69). To keep it in good shape, shorten leggy growths in early spring and remove flowering shoots to encourage growth from lower down.

H: to 5m (15ft); **S**: to 4m (12ft)
❄❄❄ ◊ ◖ ☼ ☀ ☀

Malus 'Golden Hornet'

When this flowering and fruiting ornamental crab apple is young, remove lower branches in winter to encourage a good shape. On an older tree, remove dead or diseased wood immediately, and cut off any branches causing an obstruction.

H: 10m (30ft); **S**: 8m (25ft)
❄❄❄ ◊ ◖ ☼ ☀

Malus hupehensis

This is an ornamental flowering and fruiting apple tree. When it is young, remove lower branches in winter to encourage a good shape. Remove dead or diseased branches on old plants at any time, and cut off any others that are out of place.

H: 12m (40ft); **S**: 12m (40ft)
❄❄❄ ◊ ◖ ☼ ☀ ▽

Nandina domestica
This evergreen, clump-forming shrub has white flowers during the summer followed by berries in the autumn. It requires minimal pruning to maintain its shape – remove the oldest stems in the summer. Over-pruning reduces the number of flowers produced.

H: 2m (6ft); **S**: 1.5m (5ft)
❄❄ ◌ ◑ ☼ ⚲

Olearia stellulata
The daisy bush is a compact, free-flowering evergreen shrub that is covered in white flowers in late spring. Hard prune leggy, untidy specimens immediately after flowering has finished.

H: 2m (6ft); **S**: 2m (6ft)
❄❄ ◌ ☼

Osmanthus heterophyllus '*Variegatus*'
An evergreen compact shrub with small, fragrant white flowers and holly-like leaves, used for hedging or topiary (*see pp.112–117*). Prune hedges in late spring or early summer, and clip topiary in the summer.

H: 5m (15ft); **S**: 5m (15ft)
❄❄ ◌ ☼ ☼

Parthenocissus tricuspidata
Boston ivy is a vigorous self-clinging climber that is grown for its attractive autumn foliage colours, which range from brilliant red to purple. Prune in spring before it comes into leaf or autumn after leaf fall to maintain its shape and keep it in check.

H: 20m (70ft)
❄❄❄ ◌ ◑ ☼ ☼ ⚲

Perovskia '*Blue Spire*'
This is an attractive compact shrub with blue flowers in the late summer and attractive silvery foliage. Prune annually in spring, cutting back the stems to 15cm (6in) to encourage strong growths, which will flower during the forthcoming summer.

H: 1.2m (4ft); **S**: 1m (3ft)
❄❄❄ ◌ ☼ ⚲

Philadelphus
Mock orange is grown for its white, highly scented flowers, which appear in early summer. Hard prune the shrub to 15cm (6in) in early spring every three or four years, or remove one-third of the oldest stems annually after flowering (*see p.57*).

H: to 3m (10ft); **S**: to 2.5m (8ft)
❄❄❄ ◌ ◑ ☼ ☼ ⚲

Plant pruning guide (Ph–Rh)

Photinia x fraseri 'Red Robin'

An evergreen shrub that has attractive bright red new growths and can be grown as a freestanding shrub or decorative hedge. If grown as a hedge, trim in late summer; a freestanding plant should be shaped in early spring.

H: 5m (15ft); **S**: 5m (15ft)
❄❄❄ ◌ ◗ ☼ ☽ ♉

Phygelius x rectus 'African Queen'

This plant has long tubular orange flowers during the summer. To prevent the plant becoming leggy, treat it like a perennial, cutting back all the stems to almost ground level in the spring.

H: 1.5m (5ft); **S**: 1.5m (5ft)
❄❄ ◌ ◗ ☼ ♉

Physocarpus opulifolius 'Dart's Gold'

An attractive clump-forming shrub with bright yellow new foliage, it produces white flowers in early summer. Little pruning is required, except to remove any of the outer stems that are spoiling its shape.

H: 2m (6ft); **S**: 2.5m (8ft)
❄❄❄ ◌ ◗ ☼ ☽ ♉

Pittosporum tenuifolium

Many of the forms of this evergreen shrub have variegated foliage and it makes an attractive formal focal point. The only pruning required is to retain the plant's symmetry by lightly trimming it in late spring.

H: 4–10m (12–30ft); **S**: 2–5m (6–15ft)
❄❄ ◌ ◗ ☼ ☽ ♉

Potentilla fruticosa 'Goldfinger'

An attractive small shrub with golden flowers during the summer, this pretty shrubby potentilla requires just a light trim in early spring to maintain its rounded shape.

H: 1m (3ft); **S**: 1.5m (5ft)
❄❄❄ ◌ ☼

Prunus avium 'Plena'

This ornamental cherry has large white flowers in mid-spring. Prune in early summer to reduce the risk of infection. Remove dead, diseased, or crossing branches. Young trees should be pruned at the same time.

H: 12m (40ft); **S**: 12m (40ft)
❄❄❄ ◌ ◗ ☼ ♉

Prunus laurocerasus

Cherry laurel is an evergreen with glossy green leaves. Prune freestanding shrubs in early spring to reduce their size, and a hedge in early autumn. Use secateurs, as shearing shreds the leaves. Prune overgrown plants to just above the ground in spring.

H: 8m (25ft); **S**: 10m (30ft)
❄❄❄ ◌ ◗ ☼ ☼ ☀ ♉

Prunus mume

This attractive, early flowering ornamental cherry blossoms on last year's shoots. In early summer, reduce the length of all main branches by 30cm (12in) to encourage new growths, which will be covered in flowers the following spring.

H: 9m (28ft); **S**: 9m (28ft)
❄❄❄ ◌ ◗ ☼

Prunus serrula

The attractive mahogany-red bark on this ornamental cherry makes an eye-catching feature in winter. In early summer, remove the lower branches of a young tree to give at least 1.8m (6ft) of clear trunk. Remove dead and diseased branches as seen.

H: 10m (30ft); **S**: 10m (30ft)
❄❄❄ ◌ ◗ ☼ ♉

Pyracantha 'Orange Glow'

Firethorn is an evergreen shrub or small tree grown for its orange autumn and winter fruits. It can be grown against a wall, as a hedge, or as a freestanding shrub. Prune in spring to maintain its shape, taking care not to remove flower buds.

H: 3m (10ft); **S**: 3m (10ft)
❄❄❄ ◌ ☼ ☼ ☀ ♉

Pyrus salicifolia *var.* orientalis 'Pendula'

This attractive silver-leaved weeping pear has creamy-white flowers and small brown, inedible fruits. Remove the lower branches of a young tree in winter to create a clear stem for the weeping branches to cascade down.

H: 5m (15ft); **S**: 4m (12ft)
❄❄❄ ◌ ☼ ♉

Rhamnus alaternus 'Argenteovariegata'

Prune this fast-growing evergreen shrub in early spring to remove any leggy growths and to maintain the shape of the bush. If any stems with all-green leaves appear, remove them without delay.

H: 5m (15ft); **S**: 4m (12ft)
❄❄ ◌ ☼ ♉

Plant pruning guide (Rh–Ro)

Rhamnus frangula (*syn.* Frangula alnus 'Aspleniifolia')
In the autumn, alder buckthorn has attractive yellow foliage and ornamental berries. The shrub responds well to being hard pruned to almost ground level every three or four years.

H: 3–4m (10–12ft); **S**: 2–3m (6–10ft)
❄❄❄ ◐ ◑ ☼ ◑

Rhododendron luteum
This deciduous, clump-forming azalea is grown for its attractive yellow, scented flowers in early summer and its autumn foliage colour. It normally requires very little pruning, but you can hard prune overgrown plants to almost ground level in early spring.

H: 4m (12ft); **S**: 4m (12ft)
❄❄❄ ◊ ◐ ☼ ◑ ♈

Rhododendron *Nobleanum Group*
Most hybrid rhododendrons require little or no pruning, although plants that have rough bark, such as those in the Nobleanum Group, can be pruned in early spring if they are too large. They will regenerate.

H: 5m (15ft); **S**: 5m (15ft)
❄❄❄ ◊ ◐ ☼ ◑

Rhododendron 'Rose Bud'
This attractive evergreen azalea normally requires very little pruning. However, it can be trained into formal shapes and also makes an attractive, low-growing hedge. In early summer, after flowering has finished, lightly trim with shears.

H: to 90cm (36in); **S**: to 90cm (36in)
❄❄❄ ◊ ◐ ☼

Rhus typhina
A deciduous shrub or small tree, the stag's horn sumach has attractive divided foliage, which turns a brilliant orange-red in the autumn. Hard prune it in early spring to keep compact: cut the stems back to between 30–60cm (12–24in) from the ground.

H: 5m (15ft) or more; **S**: 6m (20ft)
❄❄❄ ◊ ◐ ☼ ♈

Ribes sanguineum 'Pulborough Scarlet'
The stems of this ornamental currant bear masses of dark red, white-centred flowers in spring. To contain the plant's size and vigour, remove one-third of the oldest stems annually immediately after flowering.

H: 3m (10ft); **S**: 2.5m (8ft)
❄❄❄ ◊ ◐ ☼ ◑ ♈

Ribes speciosum
This currant is normally grown and trained against a wall or fence, and has beautiful red flowers from mid- to late spring. Remove one-third of the older stems immediately after flowering and tie the remaining stems to the wall or support.

H: 2m (6ft); **S**: 2m (6ft)
✻✻✻ ◊ ◑ ☼ ☼ ♈

Robinia pseudoacacia 'Frisia'
The main feature of this deciduous tree is its golden foliage. To produce a small golden shrub, coppice young plants every spring (*see pp.36–37*). Do not prune large trees except to remove dead or diseased wood as the wounds heal slowly.

H: 15m (50ft); **S**: 8m (25ft)
✻✻✻ ◊ ◑ ☼ ♈

Rosa *Baby Love*
This patio rose is grown for its single, clear yellow summer flowers. Prune in early spring, cutting the stems back by one-half to encourage flowering growths (*see pp.58–59*). Also remove any dead or diseased stems and crossing growths.

H: 1.2m (3½ft); **S**: 75cm (30in)
✻✻✻ ◊ ◑ ☼ ♈

Rosa 'Climbing Iceberg'
Prune climbing roses in autumn or early spring. Remove the oldest stems and spur prune the previous season's flowering growths to two or three buds to encourage more flowers in early summer (*see also pp.86–89*). Tie in any strong new stems.

H: 3m (10ft)
✻✻✻ ◊ ◑ ☼ ♈

Rosa 'Crimson Shower'
Grow this rambling rose for its rich red flowers. If trained on a support, remove some of the oldest canes in early spring and spur prune (*see pp.88–89*). When trained through a tree, you only need to cut out dead or diseased growth.

H: 2.5m (8ft); **S**: 2.2m (7ft)
✻✻✻ ◊ ◑ ☼ ♈

Rosa 'Félicité Parmentier'
This is a lovely scented, old-fashioned shrub rose. Prune in early spring, reducing the height of the plant by cutting back the main stems by one-quarter, and lightly trimming the side-shoots (*see pp.60–61*). Remove any dead, diseased, and crossing stems.

H: 1.3m (4½ft); **S**: 1.2m (4ft)
✻✻✻ ◊ ◑ ☼ ♈

Plant pruning guide (Ro–Sa)

Rosa glauca
This rose is mainly grown for its attractive blue-green foliage. To keep it tidy and to encourage strong young growths, prune in early spring by removing one-third of the older stems. Hard prune overgrown plants to about 15cm (6in) from ground level.

H: 2m (6ft); **S**: 1.5m (5ft)
❀❀❀ ◌ ◐ ☼ ♖

Rosa *Lovely Lady*
A hybrid tea rose with salmon-pink scented flowers, Lovely Lady is pruned in early spring like other hybrid tea roses. Remove all but three or four older growths, and cut these back to about 15cm (6in), ideally to an outward facing bud (*see p.62*).

H: 75cm (30in); **S**: 60cm (24in)
❀❀❀ ◌ ◐ ☼ ♖

Rosa mulliganii
Covered with white, scented flowers in the summer and red hips in the autumn, this rose will climb up supports or into trees. Remove the oldest canes in early spring and spur prune lateral growths to three buds to encourage flowers (*see pp.88–89*).

H: 6m (20ft)
❀❀❀ ◌ ◐ ☼ ♖

Rosa *Paul Shirville*
The dark reddish-green foliage of this hybrid tea rose contrasts beautifully with its fragrant rose-pink flowers, which appear from summer to autumn. Prune as for Lovely Lady (*above*) and also *see p.62*.

H: 1m (3ft); **S**: 75cm (30in)
❀❀❀ ◌ ◐ ☼ ♖

Rosa *Queen Elizabeth*
Queen Elizabeth is a pink-flowered floribunda rose that blooms from summer to autumn. Prune in early spring, leaving 6 or 8 strong stems. Cut these back to about 20-30cm (8-12in) from the ground, to an outward facing bud if possible (*see p.63*).

H: 2.2m (7ft); **S**: 1m (3ft)
❀❀❀ ◌ ◐ ☼

Rosa *Queen Mother*
Prune this floriferous, pale pink-flowered patio rose in early spring. Prune all the stems back by about one-half to encourage lots of flowering growths (*see pp.58–59*). Also remove any dead or diseased stems, and any crossing growths.

H: 40cm (16in); **S**: 60cm (24in)
❀❀❀ ◌ ◐ ☼ ♖

Rosa rugosa

This species rose has thorny stems and red, richly perfumed flowers from summer to autumn. It makes an effective hedging plant and requires minimal pruning apart from removing one or two of the oldest stems each year in late winter or early spring.

H: 1–2.5m (3–8ft); **S**: 1–2.5m (3–8ft)
❄❄❄ ◊ ◐ ☼

Rosa 'Sally Holmes'

'Sally Holmes' is a modern shrub rose that flowers from summer to autumn and needs to be pruned in early spring. Reduce its height by one-quarter and remove any dead, diseased, or crossing stems and any weak twiggy growths (see pp.60–61).

H: 2m (6ft); **S**: 1m (3ft)
❄❄❄ ◊ ◐ ☼ ♈

Rosa Trumpeter

Like Queen Elizabeth (facing page), this rose is a floribunda. It is appreciated for its clusters of vivid orange-red flowers that brighten up beds and borders from summer to autumn. Prune as for Queen Elizabeth (see also p.63).

H: 60cm (24in); **S**: 50cm (20in)
❄❄❄ ◊ ◐ ☼ ♈

Rosmarinus officinalis

This aromatic herb has small, silvery evergreen leaves and blue flowers in late spring. Old plants do not respond well to hard pruning and are best replaced. Shear young plants in early summer after the flowers have faded to maintain an even shape.

H: 1.5m (5ft); **S**: 1.5m (5ft)
❄❄ ◊ ◐ ☼

Rubus cockburnianus

Grow this thorny decorative bramble for its winter interest when the stems are covered in brilliant white bloom. Prune to almost ground level annually in early spring to encourage strong growths. Take care when cutting this shrub because the thorns are vicious.

H: 2.5m (8ft); **S**: 2.5m (8ft)
❄❄❄ ◊ ☼

Salix alba var. vitellina 'Britzensis'

The attractive orange-yellow stems make this form of white willow a must for winter interest. Coppice or pollard all shoots, first removing weak, dead, or diseased growth, to two or three pairs of healthy buds (see pp.36–39).

H: 25m (80ft) if unpruned; **S**: 10m (30ft) ❄❄❄ ◊ ◐ ◖ ☼ ♈

Plant pruning guide (Sa–Sy)

Salix daphnoides
Violet willow is grown for winter interest when the stems are covered in white bloom. Grey catkins follow. Prune hard in spring, cutting strong branches back to two or three pairs of buds from the ground. Remove all weak, dead, or diseased stems.

H: 8m (25ft); **S**: 6m (20ft)
❄❄❄ ◊ ◊ ☼

Sambucus nigra 'Aurea'
This ornamental elder is grown for its white flowers, ornamental fruit, and golden yellow leaves. Prune annually in early spring – cut back all its stems to two or three buds of the previous year's growth, to leave a structure similar to Cotinus (see pp. 48–49).

H: 6m (20ft); **S**: 6m (20ft)
❄❄❄ ◊ ◊ ☼ ☼ ♈ ♉

Santolina chaemaecyparissus
Aromatic grey foliage and bright yellow pompom flowers in the summer define this shrub. It can be grown as a low hedge or edging plant and also on its own. Trim over in spring using shears in a similar fashion to lavender (see pp.64–65).

H: 50cm (20in); **S**: 1m (3ft)
❄❄ ◊ ☼ ♉

Schizophragma hydrangeoides
This vigorous, self-clinging climber produces fragrant, creamy-white, flat-topped flowerheads in midsummer, which are set off by the dark green leaves. Its pruning requirements are the same as for Hydrangea petiolaris (see p.130).

H: 12m (40ft)
❄❄❄ ◊ ◊ ☼ ☼

Skimmia japonica 'Nymans'
A useful evergreen shrub with scented flowers that appear in mid- to late spring followed by red berries. It requires minimal pruning apart from occasionally shortening some shoots to maintain its shape.

H: 6m (20ft); **S**: 6m (20ft)
❄❄❄ ◊ ◊ ☼ ☼ ♉

Solanum crispum 'Glasnevin'
The Chilean potato tree is a vigorous, slightly tender climber grown for its scented, purple-blue summer flowers. It requires minimal pruning, but can be cut back in spring if it has outgrown its situation.

H: 6m (20ft)
❄❄ ◊ ◊ ☼ ♉

Sorbus commixta

A small, upright tree grown for its autumn foliage colour and red berries. Sorbus trees require little pruning apart from shaping young specimens in early summer. Remove any dead or diseased branches as soon as you see them.

H: 10m (30ft); **S**: 7m (22ft)
❋❋❋ ◊ ◑ ☼ ☀

Spiraea japonica

This is a small, deciduous clump-forming shrub with pink or white flowers which appear from mid- to late summer. It flowers on the current year's growth, so hard prune in early spring if required.

H: 2m (6ft); **S**: 1.5m (5ft)
❋❋❋ ◊ ◑ ☼

Spiraea nipponica 'Snowmound'

A fast-growing shrub, with white midsummer flowers that appear on shoots formed the previous year. To encourage these shoots, cut back one-third of the older stems to the base of the plant immediately after flowering.

H: to 2.5m (8ft); **S**: to 2.5m (8ft)
❋❋❋ ◊ ◑ ☼ ♆

Stachyurus 'Magpie'

A variegated shrub that produces pendulous stems of creamy yellow flowers in spring. It can be grown on its own or against a wall. Freestanding plants require no pruning, while those grown as wall shrubs can be pruned to shape after flowering.

H: 1–4m (3–12ft); **S**: 3m (10ft)
❋❋❋ ◊ ◑ ☼ ☀

Stewartia pseudocamellia

White flowers in summer and good autumn foliage colour distinguish this tree. It also has ornamental bark, which can be enjoyed by removing young lower branches in early spring to achieve a clear stem of up to 1.8m (6ft). No other pruning is required.

H: 20m (70ft); **S**: 8m (25ft)
❋❋❋ ◊ ☼ ☀ ♆

Syringa vulgaris

Lilac trees offer richly scented flowers from late spring to early summer. They grow without pruning, but if plants need containing, they tolerate being cut back hard every year after flowering, when some of the oldest growths can be removed.

H: 7m (22ft); **S**: 7m (22ft)
❋❋❋ ◊ ◑ ☼

Plant pruning guide (Ta–Wi)

Tamarix parviflora
Tamarisk is a delightful small tree with fine green foliage and masses of small pink flowers in late spring. As the plant ages it becomes untidy and needs pruning to maintain its shape. It flowers on the previous year's growth so prune after flowering.

H: 5m (15ft); **S**: 6m (20ft)
❄❄❄ ◊ ◔ ☼

Tamarix ramosissima 'Pink Cascade'
This form of tamarisk has fine green foliage and masses of rich pink airy flowers, which form on new shoots from late summer to early autumn. Prune in early spring, cutting back stems to maintain its shape.

H: 5m (15ft); **S**: 5m (15ft)
❄❄❄ ◊ ◔ ☼

Taxus baccata
Yew is an evergreen conifer that can be used as a hedging plant or topiary specimen, or trained into formal shapes. Prune hedges in late summer (see pp.96–97), and trim topiary and formal-shaped specimens in the summer (see pp.112–117).

H: to 20m (70ft); **S**: to 10m (30ft)
❄❄❄ ◊ ☼ ☼ ☀ ◑ ♈

Tilia cordata 'Winter Orange'
This lime tree has bright yellow foliage in the autumn. It can ultimately become a large tree, but with careful training it is ideal for pleaching (see p.10). Prune to shape in the winter.

H: 25m (90ft); **S**: 15m (50ft)
❄❄❄ ◊ ◔ ☼ ◑

Toona sinensis 'Flamingo'
A clump-forming tree grown for its bright pink new foliage, Toona also has white flowers in late summer and attractive autumn tints. Remove any frost-damaged growths in late spring, and hard prune large plants in spring, cutting back to almost ground level.

H: 15m (50ft); **S**: 10m (30ft)
❄❄❄ ◊ ☼

Trachelospermum jasminoides
An evergreen climber with sweetly scented white flowers during the summer, star jasmine prefers to grow against a sheltered wall. No routine annual pruning is required, but you can reduce its height by pruning in late spring.

H: 9m (28ft)
❄❄ ◊ ☼ ◑ ♈

Viburnum x bodnantense '*Dawn*'

Grown for it scented pink flowers that are produced during the autumn and early winter, this shrub can be left unpruned to become a large plant or kept small in size by removing one-fifth of the oldest stems to ground level in early spring.

H: 3m (10ft); **S**: 2m (6ft)
✾✾✾ ◊ ◑ ☀ ☀ ♈

Viburnum tinus '*Eve Price*'

This evergreen shrub is grown for its white flowers, which are produced from autumn to early spring. It does not require routine annual pruning, but remove damaged or diseased growths when seen. Hard prune overgrown plants in early spring.

H: 3m (10ft); **S**: 3m (10ft)
✾✾✾ ◊ ◑ ☀ ☀ ♈

Vitex agnus-castus *var.* latifolia

The chaste tree is a deciduous shrub with attractively divided foliage that sets off the spikes of lilac- to dark blue late summer flowers. Prune the previous year's growths back to two or three buds in early spring.

H: 2–8m (6–25ft); **S**: 2–8m (6–25ft)
✾✾ ◊ ☀

Vitis vinifera '*Purpurea*'

In autumn or early winter cut back this vigorous climbing grape. Spur prune all side stems to two buds from the previous season's growth (*see pp.34–35*) to leave short, stubby growths either side of the main stem. Shorten overly long stems in summer.

H: 7m (22ft)
✾✾✾ ◊ ◑ ☀ ♈

Weigela florida

A deciduous shrub grown for its tubular dark pink flowers that appear mainly from late spring to early summer. To prune, thin out and remove one-third of the oldest growths immediately after flowering in summer.

H: 2.5m (8ft); **S**: 2.5m (8ft)
✾✾✾ ◊ ☀ ☀

Wisteria sinensis

Wisteria is a vigorous climber that produces long, scented chains of flowers in late spring. In the winter, spur prune all the summer's growth back to two buds. During the summer, shorten long, leggy stems by up to two-thirds. (*See pp.78–79.*)

H: 9m (28ft) or more
✾✾✾ ◊ ◑ ☀ ☀ ♈

Pruning calendar

This easy-to-use guide shows which pruning tasks need to be carried out at different times of the year. Use it in conjunction with the step-by-step sequences and other pruning advice given earlier in the book to ensure your plants are cut and clipped to produce the very best effects. Remember, too, that taking time to clean and oil pruning tools during the quieter months will pay dividends by reducing the risk of disease entering plants through pruning wounds, and extending the life of your equipment.

Pruning calendar: spring

Spring is a busy time of the year, and there are plenty of pruning jobs to do now. The sap is rising and buds are swelling, which means that plants are more likely to thrive following a haircut.

Lightly prune mophead hydrangeas in mid-spring.

Main pruning tasks

The main pruning tasks in the spring are cutting back shrubs with winter stem interest, such as dogwood (*Cornus*), willow (*Salix*), and decorative bramble (*Rubus*).

Follow this by pruning floribunda, hybrid tea and shrub roses. You can also still prune climbing and rambler roses now if you didn't have time in the autumn.

As there are no leaves on most deciduous trees and shrubs at this time of year, you can clearly see and cut out wood damaged in winter by the cold and windy weather. Plants' skeletal forms also make it easier to identify and prune out diseased and crossing growths.

Trees to prune

Evergreens, such as *Magnolia grandiflora* and holly (*Ilex*), prefer to be pruned at this time of year, but most other trees are best pruned in summer or winter. In particular, avoid pruning trees that bleed sap profusely, such as birch (*Betula*) and walnut (*Juglans*), from mid-spring onwards.

Shrubs to prune

Prune winter-flowering shrubby honeysuckles, such as *Lonicera fragrantissima* and *Lonicera standishii*. In mid-spring, cut back heather (*Erica*), *Buddleja davidii*, early-flowering *Camellia*, witch hazel (*Hamamelis*), *Mahonia*, winter-flowering viburnum (*Viburnum* x *burkwoodii*), dogwood (*Cornus*), willow (*Salix*), and *Rubus*. In late spring, prune hydrangeas and, after flowering, forsythia.

Prune mahonias after flowering.

Climbers to prune

Prune clematis in Groups 2 and 3 in the spring, plus any long, wayward stems of climbing hydrangeas (*Hydrangea petiolaris*), and any climbing or rambling roses you missed in autumn. Also trim climbing honeysuckles (*Lonicera*), *Jasminum nudiflorum* and overgrown ivy (*Hedera*).

Hedge care

In late winter or early spring, renovate hornbeam (*Carpinus*), beech (*Fagus*), yew (*Taxus*) and holly (*Ilex*) hedges, and prune wildlife hedges before birds begin to nest. Pruning the latter also ensures that plants develop plenty of flowering shoots and, later, autumn berries for wildlife. Prune lavender (*Lavandula*) in mid-spring.

Renovate hornbeam and beech hedges in early spring.

Tie in new growth on climbing and rambling roses with soft twine.

Other jobs to do now

In spring, tie in the new, flexible stems of climbers. When pruning, you will have removed a lot of the old twining growths that helped the plants hold on to their supports, so they will now need extra help until the new stems have become more established.

Climbing and rambling roses, in particular, don't have a natural twining habit so they definitely need to be tied in. Likewise, clematis has lots of soft growth that is easily damaged by the wind if it is not secured.

Use garden twine to tie plants to their supports. If you are tying in large climbers with thicker stems, such as roses, you could use sturdy, flexible tube ties.

Pruning calendar: summer

Summer is the time to enjoy the results of your winter and spring pruning, but there are still some important jobs to do at this time of the year to keep your garden looking its best.

In early summer, prune leggy growths on spring-flowering clematis.

Main pruning tasks

Formal hedges need to be trimmed several times during the summer to keep their clean, sharp edges. Topiary should also be trimmed a few times to maintain its shape. Do not prune boundary hedges until late summer.

Deadhead roses to encourage repeat flowering, and prune late spring- and early summer-flowering shrubs immediately after they have bloomed, since next year's flowers will be on stems made this year. Also prune back any shrubs, trees, or climbers that are putting on too much growth or causing an obstruction.

Trees to prune

Summer is a good time to prune all trees, especially the stone fruits, such as cherries, flowering cherries, and plums (*Prunus*), and members of the rowan (*Sorbus*) family. These trees are prone to bacterial cankers and silver leaf, and pruning now helps to avoid these diseases. In late summer, prune espalier apple and pear trees.

Shrubs to prune

In early summer, prune *Garrya*. Shorten leggy growths on late-flowering *Camellias* after flowering has finished; if they have outgrown their situation, they can be hard pruned now. Prune spring- and early summer-flowering shrubs like *Deutzia*, *Philadelphus*, shrubby *Lonicera*, *Kolkwitzia*, and *Weigela* so they grow plenty of new stems for next year's flowers. In late summer, prune *Escallonia*.

Climbers to prune

In early summer, trim *Clematis macropetala* and *C. alpina*, and trim overgrown *C. montana*. Prune leggy growth of wisterias to help flower bud production, and ivy (*Hedera*) if you didn't prune it in spring. After flowering, cut back climbing honeysuckles (*Lonicera*) and the old flowerheads of climbing hydrangeas (*Hydrangea petiolaris*).

Hedge care

Prune all types in late summer once nests are abandoned; berrying hedges can be left until spring to provide food for wildlife. Prune formal hedges at least twice in summer. Trim lavender (*Lavandula*) hedges lightly after flowering.

Prune all stone fruits, such as *Prunus serrula*.

You can prune ivy from spring to autumn to keep it neat.

Remove diseased and damaged material as soon as you see it.

Other jobs to do now

Continue to train and tie in climbers during the summer. Climbing and rambling roses must be tied in regularly to protect long growths from wind damage, since they hold next year's flowering display. Also tie in Group 3 clematis to hold plants together, and wisteria to fill any gaps in coverage and to protect stems from wind damage.

Remove any diseased or dead growth on trees at any time. Dispose of diseased material by burning responsibly or taking it to a waste disposal site – don't compost it.

Trees can look quite different when clothed with leaves so compare them in summer and winter before deciding what to prune. Leaves weigh down branches and can block paths or views, so some stems may need removing.

Pruning calendar: autumn

Your garden is now ready to put to bed for the winter, but as you do so, take time to enjoy the firework display produced by the leaves and berries of ornamental trees, shrubs, and climbers.

Clean and oil secateurs and other tools.

Main pruning tasks

Don't prune trees and shrubs in the autumn unless it is absolutely necessary. There are many fungal spores around at this time of the year and a high risk of diseases penetrating the cut surfaces.

It is, however, a good time to prune and train climbing and rambling roses as their stems are quite flexible and easily trained now. Reduce the height of hybrid tea and floribunda roses by one-third to prevent wind rock. Catch up with any pruning that you missed or didn't have time for in the summer, such as pruning back leggy growths on wisterias. It is also an ideal time to clean and sharpen pruning tools. Then sit back and admire the foliage and fruiting displays around you.

Trees to prune

Autumn is not a good time to prune trees as fungal spores can land on pruning cuts, increasing the risk of infection.

Shrubs to prune

Although most pruning jobs are best left until late winter or early spring, you should reduce the height of hybrid tea and floribunda roses by one-third to prevent their stems from rocking in winter winds and damaging the main stem and roots. Also remove *Buddleja* flowerheads and the top one-third of the shoots to prevent the plant self-seeding. Do not remove spent hydrangea flowerheads as they help to protect developing flower shoots from frost, and also provide attractive architectural structure in winter. Seedheads, fruits and berries that are left on shrubs now have both wildlife and decorative value.

Trees are prone to infections in autumn so do not prune them.

Climbers to prune

Autumn is the ideal time to prune climbing and rambling roses. These plants still have sap in their stems, which makes them pliable and easy to train onto their supports. If the job is left until winter, the stems lose their flexibility and are more likely to snap. You can also prune Virginia creeper and Boston ivy (*Parthenocissus*) after leaf fall.

Hedge care

Any hedges not pruned in summer can be cut back now, but do not prune wildlife hedges, which are best left until spring, as their fruit and berries provide food for birds and other wildlife through the colder months.

Prune the climber *Parthenocissus* after leaf drop.

Other jobs to do now

The autumn is tidying-up time. Cover trees or shrubs that need frost protection, such as palms, tree ferns, and fruits like apricots. Leave the fronds on tree ferns and palms as they protect plants from frost. For further protection, tie them together over the crown.

As the leaves fall, the basic structure of plants becomes more visible, and you will be able to see more clearly what needs to be pruned in spring. Rake up fallen leaves and fruit, such as apples, and use to make compost and leaf mould, which you can later spread under pruned plants to feed and mulch them.

If you have any logs left from pruning in the summer, you could construct a log pile, which benefits wildlife.

Cover tender plants with fleece to protect them against frost.

Pruning calendar: winter

In winter, you can really appreciate the form, shape, and silhouette of the trees in your garden, while the stem colour of many woody plants is another boon to otherwise slumbering beds and borders.

On wisterias, spur prune the stems you cut back in the summer.

Main pruning tasks

Late winter or early spring is a good time to hard prune overgrown shrubs, which are dormant at this time of the year. You can also see clearly the structure and naked silhouettes of trees, making them easier to prune. Summer is the ideal time to prune many trees, but winter is sometimes better because you may have more time to do the job properly. However, do not prune cherries and plums (*Prunus*), or members of the rowan (*Sorbus*) family.

You can also now admire the results of your earlier pruning efforts, with the attractive trunks and stems of trees and shrubs like the snake-bark maple (*Acer davidii*), birch (*Betula*), cherry (*Prunus serrula*), and dogwood (*Cornus*) creating stunning winter features.

Trees to prune

This is a good time to prune a wide range of trees and shrubs (with the exception of stone fruits) as you can clearly identify crossing branches and diseased wood. Prune trees with ornamental bark, such as *Acer davidii* and *Acer griseum* and birches. Apple and pear trees should also be pruned in winter.

Shrubs to prune

Prune any large or overgrown shrubs, such as *Mahonia* or *Philadelphus*, which can be cut back hard now or in early spring. You may lose the coming year's flowers by hard pruning, but the plant will recover the following year.

Climbers to prune

Spur prune wisteria in the winter, as the buds are not swelling and so less likely to be damaged. Also tackle *Actinidia* and Virginia creeper (*Parthenocissus*), and renovate overgrown ivies (*Hedera*). Remove long growths from around doors and window frames, and also where they have invaded gutters and grown under roof tiles. Shorten the main stems of all overly tall climbers, such as *Hydrangea petiolaris*.

Hedge care

Winter is the time for renovation work, reducing the height and width of overgrown hedges. Brush off snow from flat-topped hedges as its weight can damage their structure. Leave the crisp, bronzed foliage on hornbeam and beech hedges in the winter months because it adds ornamental value and also makes an excellent windbreak.

Prune apple trees in winter when their structure is more visible.

Brush snow off the top of hedges to prevent structural damage.

Fresh foliage and berries make wonderful seasonal wreaths.

Other jobs to do now

Tie in anything that needs to be supported. At the same time, check that ties and supports have not been damaged during storms, or become too tight around stems and trunks. Bring berries and evergreen branches into the house for festive winter decorations.

You can dispose of pruning material (and old Christmas trees) in a variety of ways. Shred the woody bits to make a valuable mulching material, and compost soft growth. Burning material is an alternative method, but can be antisocial if you live near other houses. Alternatively, take all your off-cuts to your local waste disposal site, along with any diseased material, if you do not plan to burn it.

Index

A

Abelia x grandiflora 120
Acer (maple)
  A. davidii (snake-bark
    maple) 120, 154, 155
  A. griseum 155
  A. palmatum 120
  A. 'White Tigress' (snake-
    bark maple) 16, 17
Actinidia deliciosa (kiwi)
  120, 155
alder buckthorn see
  Rhamnus frangula
apples 18, 19, 72–5
  espaliers 18, 19
  winter pruning 155
  see also Malus
arches 94
Artemisia 'Powis Castle' 120
Aucuba japonica 54, 120
autumn tasks 152–3

B

bark, showing off 13, 16–17
bay laurel see Laurus nobilis
bay, standard 12, 13
beauty bush see Kolkwitzia
  amabilis
beech see Fagus
bell heather see Erica
  cinerea
Berberis 93
  B. darwinii 93
  B. x stenophylla 121
  B. thunbergii 41, 121
berries, pruning for 9, 153
Betula (birch) 149, 154, 155
  B. utilis var. jacquemontii
    16, 121
  removing lower branches
    13, 16
birch see Betula
blueberries 18
bonsai scissors 41
borders, informal pruning 9
Boston ivy see
  Parthenocissus tricuspidata
box see Buxus
box-leaved holly see Ilex
  crenata

branches
  crossing and rubbing 28
  removal 32–3
  torn 32
  twin leaders 29
broom, Mount Etna see
  Genista aetnensis
bud indentification 30–1
Buddleja davidii (butterfly
  bush) 121, 149, 153
butterfly bush see Buddleja
  davidii
Buxus (box) 93
  B. sempervirens 93, 98–9,
    121
  parterre 10
  shearing 31, 98–9
  standard formation 110
  topiary 41, 112–17

C

california lilac see Ceanothus
Callistemon 21
Calluna vulgaris (common
  Scottish heather) 121
Camellia 54–5
  C. japonica 122
  C. x williamsii 'Donation'
    122
  spring pruning 149
  summer pruning 151
Campsis x tagliabuana 122
canopies 10
Carpinus (hornbeam) 10, 92,
  93
  C. betulus 122
  dead wood 29
  renovating 102–5
  shaping 94
  spring pruning 149
Caryopteris x clandonensis
  'Arthur Simmonds' 122
Catalpa bignonioides 48, 122
Ceanothus (California lilac)
  56–7
  C. 'Blue Mound' 123
  C. 'Puget Blue', informal
    pruning 9
Ceratostigma willmottianum
  123
Cercis canadensis 'Forest
  Pansy' 123

Chaenomeles cultivars
  (flowering quince) 123
chain saws 27
Chamaecyparis lawsoniana
  (Lawson cypress) 93
chaste tree see Vitex agnus-
  castus
cherry see Prunus
Chimonanthus praecox 123
Choisya (Mexican orange
  blossom)
  C. 'Aztec Pearl' 9
  C. ternata 123
Christmas decorations 155
Cistus (rock rose), C.
  'Grayswood Pink' 20, 21
Clematis 80–3
  C. alpina 80, 124, 151
  C. armandii 80, 124
  C. 'Etoile Violette' 80, 124
  C. 'Frances Rivis' 80
  C. 'H.F. Young' 80, 124
  C. 'Jackmanii' 124
  C. x jouiniana 82
  C. macropetala 151
  C. montana 21, 80
    encouraging flowering 15
    summer pruning 151
  C. 'Nelly Moser' 80, 124
  C. tangutica 80, 83
  texensis type 80
  viticella type 80
climbers 76–89
  autumn pruning 153
  spring pruning 149
  summer pruning 151
  tying in 149
  winter pruning 155
  see also specific climbers
    e.g. Wisteria
cloud pruning 40
colour, pruning for 9, 16–17
cone shapes 112, 114–15
conifers
  shaping 94
  topiary 112
  trimming and shaping, 40-1
Convulvulus cneorum 21
coppicing 36–7
coral spot 29
Cornus (dogwood) 148
  C. alba 125

C. alternifolia 'Variegata'
  125
C. kousa var. chinensis 125
C. sanguinea 'Winter
  Beauty' 125
C. stolonifera 'Flaviramea'
  16, 17
coppicing 36–7
cutting opposite buds 31
spring pruning 149
winter pruning 154
Corylus avellana 'Contorta'
  125
Cotinus (smoke bush) 48–9
  C. coggygria 48, 125
Cotoneaster horizontalis 126
Crataegus monogyna
  (hawthorn) 93, 126
x Cupressocyparis leylandii 93
currant see Ribes
cypress
  Lawson see Chamaecyparis
    lawsoniana
  Leyland see x
    Cupressocyparis leylandii
Cytisus x praecox (broom) 126

D

Daboecia cantabrica f. alba
  126
daisy bush see Olearia
  stellulata
Daphne
  D. bholua 126
    D. b. 'Jacqueline Postill'
      42–3
  D. x burkwoodii 21
  D. cneorum 21
dead wood 29
deadheading 29, 58, 64, 68
Deutzia 151
  D. x hybrida 'Mont Rose'
    126
diseased wood 29, 151
dogwood see Cornus

E

Edgeworthia 21
Elaeagnus
  E. x ebbingei 93
  E. pungens 54, 127

Erica (heather) 149
  E. arborea 54
    E. a. var. *alpina* 127
  E. carnea 127
  E. cinerea f. *alba* (bell
    heather) 127
Escallonia 54, 151
  E. 'Apple Blossom' 127
  E. rubra 93
espaliers 18, 19
Eucalyptus gunnii 127
Euonymus
  E. europaeus 128
  E. fortunei 66, 128
  reversion, pruning out 28
Exochorda x *macrantha* 'The
  Bride' 128

F

Fagus (beech) 93, 100–1
  renovating 102–5
  spring pruning 149
x *Fatshedera lizei* 128
Fatsia japonica 54
firethorn *see Pyracantha*
flowering, pruning to
  encourage 14–15, 29, 42–3,
  58, 63
formal pruning 10–11
Forsythia x *intermedia*
  'Lynwood Variety' 128, 149
Fothergilla major 21
Fremontodendron
  'California Glory' 128
frost damage 29
frost protection 153
fruit, pruning for 18–19
fruit trees, summer pruning
  151
Fuchsia
  F. magellanica 93, 129
  standard formation 110

G

Garrya elliptica 66, 151
  G. e. 'James Roof' 129
Gaultheria mucronata 129
Genista aetnensis (Mount
  Etna broom) 129
globe shape 116–17
gloves 27

goggles 27
grape *see Vitis*
Griselinia littoralis 93, 129

H

x *Halimiocistus* 21
Hamamelis (witch hazel)
  50–1, 149
  H. x *intermedia* 'Pallida' 129
hawthorn *see Crataegus*
heather *see Erica*
  common Scottish *see*
    Calluna vulgaris
  shearing 31
Hedera (ivy) 85, 149, 151, 155
  H. helix 130
hedge trimmer
  electric 25
    safety 27
  petrol 25
hedges 90–105
  autumn pruning 153
  parterre 10, 11
  shapes 94–5
  spring pruning 149
  summer pruning 150, 151
  winter pruning 155
holly *see Ilex*
hornbeam *see Carpinus*
Hydrangea
  frost damage 29
  H. arborescens 'Grandiflora'
    130
  H. macrophylla 46, 130
    H. m. 'Libelle' 29
  H. paniculata 46, 130
  H. petiolaris 130, 149, 151
  spring pruning 149
  summer pruning 151
Hypericum
  H. 'Hidcote' 130
    informal pruning 9

I

Ilex (holly) 70–1, 149
  I. aquifolium 93
  I. a. 'Pyramidalis
    Aureomarginata' 131
  I. crenata (box-leaved holly)
    131
  spring pruning 149

standard formation 110–11
Indigofera heterantha 131
informal pruning 8–9
Itea ilicifolia 131
ivy *see Hedera*

J, K

Jasminum (jasmine)
  J. nudiflorum (winter
    jasmine) 131, 149
  J. officinale (common
    jasmine) 131
Juglans (walnut) 149
Kerria japonica '*Golden
  Guinea*' 132
kiwi *see Actinidia deliciosa*
Kolkwitzia 151
  K. amabilis 'Pink Cloud'
    (beauty bush) 132

L

Laburnum 21
ladders 27
Laurus nobilis (bay laurel) 132
Lavandula (lavender) 64–5,
  93, 149
  L. angustifolia 132
  shearing 31, 64–5
  summer pruning 151
  trimming and shaping 41
Lavatera x *clementii* 'Barnsley'
  (mallow) 132
Lawson cypress *see*
  Chamaecyparis lawsoniana
leaders, twin 29
leaf
  effects, encouraging 48
  pruning out reversion 28
Lespedeza thunbergii 132
Leycesteria formosa 133
Leyland cypress *see* x
  Cupressocyparis leylandii
Ligustrum
  L. ovalifolium 93
  L. lucidum 133
lilac *see Syringa vulgaris*
lime *see Tilia*
lollipops 12, 13, 116–17
Lonicera (honeysuckle)
  2–3, 84
  L. fragrantissima 149

L. nitida 93, 133
  L. n. 'Baggeson's Gold' 9
  topiary 112
L. periclymenum 'Graham
  Thomas' 133
L. standishii 149
L. x *purpusii* 133
  L. x *p.* 'Winter Beauty'
    52–3
spring pruning 149
summer pruning 151
loppers 25
long-armed 25
Luma apiculata 133

M

Magnolia
  M. grandiflora 134, 149
  M. x *loebneri* 'Leonard
    Messel' 134
Mahonia 68–9, 149
  M. aquifolium 134
  M. x *media* 'Charity' 134
  spring pruning 149
  winter pruning 155
mallow *see Lavatera* x
  clementii
Malus hupehensis (apple)
  134
maple *see Acer*
Mexican orange blossom
  see Choisya
mock orange *see*
  Philadelphus
Mount Etna broom *see*
  Genista aetnensis

N

Nandina domestica 135
neighbouring plants,
  pruning law 27
no-prune shrubs and trees
  20–1

O

old wood pruning 30
Olearia stellulata (daisy
  bush) 135
Osmanthus heterophyllus
  'Variegatus' 135

Index

P, Q

parterre 10, 11
Parthenocissus (Virginia creeper) 153, 155
  P. tricuspidata (Boston ivy) 135
peacock shape 113
pear, weeping *see Pyrus salicifolia*
pears 18, 19
Perovskia 'Blue Spire' 135
Philadelphus (mock orange) 56–7, 135, 151, 155
  P. 'Belle Etoile' 15
Photinia x *fraseri* 'Red Robin' 136
Phygelius x *rectus* 'African Queen' 136
Physocarpus opulifolius 'Dart's Gold' 136
Pieris, P. floribunda 21
Pittosporum tenuifolium 136
platforms with ladders 27
pleaching 10
pollarding 38–9
Potentilla fruticosa 'Goldfinger' 136
Prostanthera 21
Prunus (cherry)
  P. avium 'Plena' 136
  P. laurocerasus (cherry laurel) 54, 93, 137
  P. lusitanica 54
  P. mume 137
  P. rufa 16, 17
  P. serrula 137, 154
  summer pruning 151
Pyracantha (firethorn)
  informal pruning 9
  P. 'Orange Glow' 137
pyramids 18, 19
Pyrus salicifolia var. *orientalis* 'Pendula' (weeping pear) 13, 137
quince, flowering *see Chaenomeles cultivars*

R

reversion, pruning out 28
Rhamnus

R. alaternus 'Argenteovariegata' 137
R. frangula (alder buckthorn) 138
Rhododendron
  R. 'Blue Diamond' 20, 21
  R. luteum 138
  R. Nobleanum Group 138
  R. 'Rose Bud' 138
Rhus
  R. chinensis 48
  R. typhina (stag's horn sumach) 48, 138
Ribes (ornamental currant)
  R. sangineum 'Pulborough Scarlet' 138
  R. speciosum 139
Robinia pseudoacacia 'Frisia' 139
rock rose *see Cistus*
Rodgersia, for underplanting 13
Rosa (rose)
  R. Alexander 62
  R. 'Arthur Bell' 63
  R. Baby Love 139
  R. 'Blanche Double de Coubert' 62
  R. 'Blessings' 62
  R. 'Boule de Neige' 62
  R. 'Charles de Mills' 62
  R. 'Climbing Iceberg' 139
  R. 'Climbing Mrs Sam McGredy' 15
  R. 'Crimson Shower' 139
  R. Dawn Chorus 62
  R. 'De Rescht' 62
  R. 'Deep Secret' 62
  R. Elina 62
  R. 'English Miss' 63
  R. 'Fantin-Latour' 62
  R. Fascination 62
  R. 'Félicité Parmentier' 139
  R. Fellowship 62
  R. 'Fragrant Delight' 63
  R. 'Frau Dagmar Hartopp' 62
  R. Freedom 62
  R. glauca 140
  R. Iceberg 62
  R. Ingrid Bergman 62
  R. 'Just Joey'' 62

R. 'Louise Odier' 62
R. Lovely Lady 62, 140
R. 'Madame Isaac Pereire' 62
R. 'Madame Pierre Oger' 62
R. 'Maiden's Blush' 62
R. Memento 62
R. mulliganii 108–9
R. mundi 62
R. Paul Shirville 62, 140
R. Peace 62
R. Pretty Lady 62
R. 'Princess of Wales' 63
R. Queen Elizabeth 63, 140
R. Queen Mother 140
R. Remember Me 62
R. Remembrance 62
R. rugosa 62, 92, 93, 141
  R. r. 'Alba' 62
R. 'Sally Holmes' 141
R. Savoy Hotel 62
R. Sexy Rexy 63
R. 'Silver Jubilee' 62
R. 'Souvenir de la Malmaison' 62
R. Sunset Boulevard 63
R. Tall Story 63
R. Tequila Sunrise 62
R. The Times Rose 63
R. Troika 62
R. Trumpeter 63, 141
R. Warm Wishes 62
R. 'White Cockade' 86
R. 'William Lobb' 62
roses 86–9
  alternate buds 31
  autumn pruning 152, 153
  cladding 10, 11
  climbing 86–9, 108–9
    autumn pruning 152–3
    encouraging flowering 15
    spring pruning 149
    spur pruning 35
  deadheading 29, 58, 150
  floribunda 63
  hedges 92
  hybrid tea 62
  informal pruning 8
  Old garden 62
  patio 58–9
  rambling 88–9, 108–9
    autumn pruning 152–3

  informal pruning 9
  spring pruning 149
  rope swags 108–9
  shoot buds 30–1
  shrub 60–1
  spring pruning 148–9
  on tripods 86–7
  tying in 149, 151
Rosmarinus officinalis (rosemary) 141
Rubus (bramble) 148, 149
  R. cockburnianus 16, 141
Ruscus 21

S

safety
  branch removal 33
  hedge cutting 96–7
  tools 26–7
Salix (willow)
  pollarding 38–9
  S. alba var. *vitellina* 'Britzensis' 141
  S. daphnoides (violet willow) 141
  spring pruning 148, 149
Salvia (golden)
  golden, informal pruning 9
Sambucus nigra (elder) 48
  S. n. 'Aurea' 142
Santolina
  informal pruning 9
  S. chamaecyparissus 142
  trimming and shaping 41
Sarcococca 21
saw
  bow 24
  chain 27
  long-armed 24
  pruning 24
    cleaning 26
    using 31
Schizophragma hydrangeoides 142
scissors for topiary pruning 41
secateurs 24
  cleaning 26
  topiary 41, 112
shaping 106–17
  see also topiary
shearing 41, 64–5
  topiary 112

shears 31
  topiary 41, 112
shoots, identification 30–1
shrubs 44–75
  autumn pruning 153
  formal pruning 10–11
  no-prune 20–1
  spring pruning 149
  summer pruning 151
  wall 66–7
  winter pruning 155
Skimmia japonica 'Nymans'
  142
smoke bush *see Cotinus*
snake-bark maple *see under*
  Acer
snow damage 155
Solanum crispum 'Glasnevin'
  142
Sorbus (rowan)
  S. aria 10
  S. commixta 143
  summer pruning 151
spaces, pruning to create
  12–13
Spiraea
  S. japonica 143
  S. nipponica 'Snowmound'
  143
spiral shapes 116–17
spring tasks 148–9

spur pruning 34–5
Stachyurus 'Magpie' 143
stag's horn sumach *see Rhus*
  typhina
standard formation 13,
  110–11
Stewartia pseudocamellia 143
sucker removal 28
sumach, stag's horn *see Rhus*
  typhina
summer tasks 150–1
Syringa vulgaris (lilac) 143

T

Tamarix
  T. parviflora 144
  T. ramosissima 'Pink
    Cascade' 144
Taxus (yew) 96–7
  parterre 10, 11
  shaping 94
  shearing 31
  spring pruning 149
  T. baccata 93, 144
  topiary 41
templates for topiary 113
Thuja plicata 93
Tilia (lime)
  pleaching 10
  T. cordata 'Winter Orange'

144
tools 24–5
  care and safety 26–7
  sterilizing 113
  topiary 112–13
Toona sinensis 144
topiary 40–1, 150
  tools and techniques 112–17
Trachelospermum jasminoides
  144
trees 44–75
  formal pruning 10–11
  no-prune 21
  spring pruning 149
  summer pruning 151
  winter pruning 155
tying in 149, 151

V

Viburnum
  standard formation 110
  V. x bodnantense
    'Dawn' 145
  V. x burkwoodii 149
  V. plicata 93
  V. rhytidophyllum 11
  V. tinus 54
    V. t. 'Eve Price' 145

violet willow *see Salix*
  daphnoides
Virginia creeper *see*
  Parthenocissus
Vitex agnus-castus var.
  latifolia (chaste tree) 145
Vitis vinifera 'Purpurea'
  (grape) 145

W, Y

wall shrubs 66–7
walnut *see Juglans*
Weigela 151
  W. florida 145
  W. 'Praecox Variegata' 48
  W. Wine and Roses 48
willow *see Salix*
winter tasks 154–5
Wisteria 78–9
  alternate buds 31
  spur pruning 35
  summer pruning 151
  tiny-tree pruning 13
  W. sinensis 145
    encouraging flowering
      14, 15
  winter pruning 154, 155
witch hazel *see Hamamelis*
yew *see Taxus*

Acknowledgements

The publisher would like to thank the following for their kind permission to reproduce their photographs:

(Key: a-above; b-below/bottom; c-centre; l-left; r-right; t-top)

8 Alamy Images: Ian Fraser, Cothay Manor, Somerset. **11** DK Images Steve Wooster, Designer: Tom Stuart-Smith/ Homage to Le Nôtre/Chelsea Flower Show 2000 (t), Peter Anderson, designer: Tom Stuart-Smith/Chelsea Flower Show 2006.
13 DK Images: Peter Anderson, designers: Marcus Barnett and Philip Nixon/Savills Garden, Chelsea Flower Show 2006.
27 www.henchman.co.uk; Tel: 01635 299847. **40** DK Images: Steve Wooster: designers: Arne Maynard and Piet Oudolf/ Evolution/Chelsea Flower Show 2000.
84 Sarah Cuttle (tr) (br); Jacqui Dracup (bl). **114** Garden Picture Library: Marie O'Hala, Bourton House, Glostershire.

All other images © Dorling Kindersley
For further information see:
www.dkimages.com

Dorling Kindersley would like to thank the garden staff at RHS Garden Wisley for their expertise and help.